About the Author

Ian Baillie was born in Birmingham in 1949. He and Kathy, his wife of forty years, have one married son, Alex. Ian took to writing light-hearted verse about historical characters to entertain and educate Alex ... and it did!

Dedication

To my wife Kathy who never lost faith or patience – trying to be funny isn't always amusing! And to my special son Alex who inspires me.

Ian Baillie

STUFF & NONSENSE:
KINGS & QUEENS

AUSTIN MACAULEY
PUBLISHERS LTD.

A CIP catalogue record for this title is available from the British Library.

ISBN 978 1 78455 923 6 (Paperback)
ISBN 978 1 78455 924 3 (Hardback)

www.austinmacauley.com

First Published (2015)
Austin Macauley Publishers Ltd.
25 Canada Square
Canary Wharf
London
E14 5LB

Printed and bound in Great Britain

Acknowledgments

To my dear friend and editor David J England without whose research, encouragement and good sense this work would never have come to fruition.

To Carlos Diaz whose artistic skills effortlessly produced the charming caricatures which serve to bring the characters to life.

Stuff & Nonsense

Kings & Queens

What do you know of our Monarchs?

Learn here of their life and times

I promise, forsooth, every word shall be truth

Providing, of course, that it rhymes!

William the Conqueror [1]

(1027 – 1087)
(r.1066 – 1087)

Willie came from Normandy
You can see it at a glance
Forty leagues at most from the southern coast
In the northern part of France

He'd grown to be a violent man
Devoid of all compassion
This uncouth ape loved pillage and rape
Then the height of fashion

He'd boast that he was civilised
A diplomat and fair
Don't be fooled, the man was cruel
With hate and bile to spare

The grapevine whispered o'er the sea
"England's Crown is free"
Will said; "Right! – I don't need an invite
That Throne is made for me!"

But when they chose someone called Harold [2]
Will was mad – fit to burst!
"I'm still coming"; he roared, "I'll not be ignored
I'm Storming Norman the First" [3]

Harold donned his new armour
Which his mum said he'd looked grand in
With troops galore he made camp by the shore
Ready to stop Will's landing

Will didn't arrive as expected
(In June of ten sixty six)
There were ocean swells; he'd run out of Quells
A damp lawn made him feel sick

The delay worked in Willie's favour
'Cos Harold had more than one foe
When Norwegian Hardrada attacked in the north [4]
"Aitch" and his troops had to go

Their armies met at Stamford Bridge [5]
A gruelling march away!
But Harold's tough mob had an eye for the job
Hardrada was soft as clay

Whilst still celebrating his victory
Bad news reached Harold's ear
The sea had improved: Willie had moved
And was settling in over here

By the time Harold got back to Sussex
His men were out on their feet
They took their stance but stood little chance
(This was before Shredded Wheat!)

And so to The Battle of Hastings [6]
They were even – it looked like a tie
'Til, distressed and jaded, Harold's men faded
And an arrow plopped in his eye

Anglo-Saxons had to go
Often with cruel dispassion [7]
Now Norman traditions filled Lordly positions
In feudalistic fashion

For knowledge of Willie's England
To understand how things were planned
You just have to look at The Domesday Book
A survey of people and land [8]

Willie demanded obedience
Devotion – nothing less
Thus he laid the foundation for a proud English Nation
With power, wealth and success

In the thick of battle at sixty
This warrior had got a touch slow
While fighting in France a foe took his chance
It's the way he'd have wanted to go!

Stuff about William I

1. William was known as "The Conqueror" from the 13th Century onwards(i)
2. Harold, was in fact King Harold II Godwinson (second son of Godwin) and he lived from around 1020 until his defeat in 1066. His father, Edward the Confessor, on his death bed, chose Harold as his successor and he was crowned in January 1066. Harold had, however, in 1064 or 1065, sworn (under duress?) to support William (later William I) as next to succeed. (i)
3. General H. Norman Schwarzkopf, also known as "Storming' Norman" was a retired United States Army 4 Star General who, while he served as Commander-in-Chief of US Central Command, was commander of the Coalition Forces in the Gulf War of 1991.(ii) He died in December 2012.
4. Harald Hardrada was the King of Norway, "the thunderbolt from the North", known for his frightening size (6 feet 4 inches), legendary cruelty, and battle experience, joined in allegiance with Tostig, Harold's estranged brother to attack Harold. (iii)
5. The Battle of Stamford Bridge took place in Yorkshire on 25th September 1066 and Harold defeated the combined forces of his brother, Tostig, and Harald Hardrada. (i)
6. William, Duke of Normandy, landed at Pevensey, near Hastings in Sussex, England, on 28th September 1066 while Harold was still occupied in the North (see Stuff 5 above). After a day long, intermittent, struggle on 14th October 1066, William was victorious and Harold dead, at The Battle of Hastings. (iv)
7. After the battle Harold's body was so badly mutilated that it could only be identified by his mistress, Edith Swan-Neck, who recognised it "... by marks on the body known only to her ...". (iii)
8. "The Domesday" Book, is a highly detailed record of English landholdings begun by William around 1085 for taxation purposes. Considered as definitive as The Book of Judgment it was, by the 1170's, known as "The Domesday Book". (iv)

More Stuff about William I

(i) Gardiner, Juliet, Ed; The History Today Who's Who in British History; Collins and Brown; London; 2000;
(ii) http://en.wikipedia.org/wiki/Norman_Schwarzkopf,_Jr. accessed 21st January 2008;
(iii) Schama, S; A History of Britain (3000 BC – AD 1603); BBC Worldwide Limited; London; 2000;
(iv) Gardiner, Juliet and Wenborn, N, Eds; The History Today Companion to British History; Collins and Brown; London; 1995.

C. Díaz

WILLIAM II
William Rufus [1]

(1058 – 1100)
(r.1087 – 1100)

Strong willed Will had left a will
From which resentment grew
Robert, the eldest of three, got Normandy [2]
His second was crowned "William Two"

Who was also known as "Rufus"
With a sobriquet of "The Red"
From his frequent ire or hair of fire?
Like a sunset on his head

The people were awfully wary
He'd had a dreadful press
"Could this lad be as cruel as his dad?"
– Sadly, the answer's "Yes!"

He ploughed his own bleak furrow
Ignoring scribes and sages
He didn't do nice, encouraged vice
And epitomised Dark Ages [3]

He'd a deep disregard for religion [4]
Hereunder you'll find lies the truth
His church visits, they say, we're not to pray
Just to nick lead off the roof!

The money was never enough
So he squeezed his subjects dry
Punitive fines, forfeits of all kinds
There was so much he wanted to buy!

Will's ending is shrouded in mystery
You'll surely be shocked to the marrow
Now see what is meant, as we proudly present
The Case of the Wayward Arrow

The scene is Brockenhurst Forest [5]
Rufus plus four – hunting game
Henry (his brother), two de Clare's and one other
Walter Tirel by name

They knew where to locate their quarry
Making straightway for the spot
Tirel spied game – carefully took aim
And fired a lethal shot

The missile sped straight past the stag
Extending the life of the brute
It would have come to a harmless ending
If Will hadn't been on its route [6] [7]

Before he'd even hit the deck
Henry pronounced him dead
Then, so we're told, before he was cold said:
"Now I can be King instead"

All players in this here drama
Ambitious, tough, pernicious
Was this freak chance? – Was it planned in advance?
To say the least – suspicious!!

Will's thirteen years lacked progress
Life in his time was torrid
He was the basest of creatures quite devoid of good features
The man was perfectly horrid! [8]

Stuff about William II

1. The name "Rufus" was derived either from his red hair or from his ruddy complexion.
2. Robert later challenged William's rule which led to revolts (1088 and 1095) and a War of Succession. (i)
3. The Dark Ages, otherwise known as the Early Middle Ages, was a period in European history from the collapse of the Roman political control in the West traditionally set in the 5th to about the late 11th Centuries. It should be emphasised, however, that the fixing of dates for the beginning and end of the Dark Ages is arbitrary, at neither time was there any sharp break in the cultural development of the continent. (Ed.)
4. The churchmen of the time considered William had a "rapacious disregard" for their property rights; Anselm, Archbishop of Canterbury was driven into exile. (i)
5. "Brockenhurst Forest" was part of what is now "The New Forest" in Hampshire, England. (Ed.)
6. The view (in "Stuff 4" above) was reflected by the chroniclers of the time, who were mainly monks, and William's death was considered God's Judgement: a view "confirmed" when the tower of Winchester Cathedral collapsed after he was buried under it. (i)
7. Coincidentally William's eldest brother, Richard, had also died in a hunting accident. (ii)
8. Notwithstanding the great deal of criticism written by monks, totally opposed to William's "worldly lifestyle" one Geoffrey Gaimar, a historian writing in 1140, albeit for the Norman aristocracy, called him "fine ... generous". (i)

More Stuff about William II

(i) Gardiner, Juliet, Ed; The History Today Who's Who in British History; Collins and Brown; London; 2000.
(ii) Sharma, S; A History of Britain (3000 BC – AD 1603); BBC Worldwide Limited; London; 2000.

HENRY I
Beauclerc [1]

(1068 – 1135)
(r.1100 – 1135)

Had Henry lurked in the wings
To lower his brother's curtain?
That scene from history's cloaked in mystery
– We'll never know for certain

We do know that brotherly love
For the Normans was sadly lacking
And here's the thing, Henry craved to be King
So he might have sent Will packing

Now, to ingratiate himself
And for a clever starter
What hit the right chords with clergy and Lords
Was The Coronation Charter [2]

This eased their lingering doubts
So they wouldn't fuss
Then he issued instructions for tax reductions
Always the magnum opus

Brother Robert returned from Crusading
Believing the Crown his by right
But his hopes went awry as Henry was sly
And Robert – not too bright!

Henry stalled his brother
Suggesting a deal would be best
Normandy for Rob, plus quite a few bob
He to stay king of the rest

Soon after when Henry saw weakness
He then provoked the affray
Rob's men were bested – Rob was arrested [3]
And never more saw light of day

Henry had twenty-nine children
Just one a legitimate male
Will: strong and fair, was groomed as his heir
One hope for his line to prevail

Father and son fought together in France
'Til Louis the Sixth was vanquished
This monocrat was Louis the Fat
– Too much mayonnaise on his sandwich!

But Henry's world was shattered
On the return cross-channel trip
An occurrence so vile – and the last time he'd smile
The wreck of his precious White Ship [4]

Three hundred knights, nobles and royals
Including the son he so cherished
Were just out of dock when the ship struck a rock
Every young soul sadly perished

Now Henry had a daughter
Matilda, after her mother
A brave young filly, who we'll call Millie [5]
To save confusion and bother

Said Henry; resigned to his loss
"Ruling's no job for a girl
But that Boadicea could generate fear
So I'll give young Millie a whirl" [6]

Millie shaped up very well
Better than most had reckoned
Then she got a nice mate – Geoff Plantagenet
And made Henry the Second

Beauclerc's demise was puzzling
A surfeit of lampreys for tea [7]
When fully loaded – he sort of imploded
Seems a bit fishy to me!

Stuff about Henry I

1. William I's third surviving son was well educated, hence his nickname which translates as "fine scholar". (i)
2. Having had himself crowned Henry feared that his brother Robert would challenge his claim to the throne. He hoped that by this charter, which overturned some of his father's oppressive measures, he would ingratiate himself with the people. (i)
3. Robert was defeated at the Battle of Tinchebrai in 1106, Henry thus gaining control of Normandy. (i)
4. The White Ship, a new vessel, set sail from Barfleur, Normandy, bound for England in 1120. Soon after leaving it struck a rock and many hundreds of lives, including that of William Adelin, Henry's only legitimate son, were lost, precipitating a dynastic crisis. (ii) The contemporary English chronicler, Orderic Vitalis, and others, have attributed the wreck to drunkenness on board. (v)
5. By marrying Matilda, in 1100, Henry strengthened his claim to the throne and his Scottish border as she was descended from Anglo-Saxon kings and sister of King Edgar of Scotland. (i)
6. Despite a second marriage (Matilda died in 1118), to Adela of Louvain, only three months after William's death in the White Ship disaster of 1120, no male heir was born and in 1127, at the Royal Council of Christmas, he made the barons swear allegiance to his daughter, The Empress Matilda, the title by which she ensured she was known throughout her life (iii)
7. Lampreys are eel-like fish with a meaty flavour but are very fatty and not easily digested. (iv) His physician had expressly forbidden them to him. (iii)

More Stuff about Henry I

(i) Gardiner, Juliet, Ed; The History Today Who's Who in British History; Collins and Brown; London; 2000.
(ii) Gardiner, Juliet, and Wenborn, N. Eds; The History Today Companion to British History; Collins and Brown; London; 1995.
(iii) Schama, S; A History of Britain (3000 BC – AD 1603); BBC Worldwide Limited; London; 2000;
(iv) http://www.quite.com/personal/cafeq/fooddeathtext1.htm;
(v) http://en.wikipedia.org/wiki/Orderic_Vitalis;

STEPHEN
Soft Steve

(1096 – 1154)
(r.1135 – 1154)

Good riddance to you Henry
You've taken your last breath
Huge rich meals of slimy eels
Brought about your death

Steven is Henry's Nephew
Henry raised him as his own [1]
And Steven signed on the dotted line [2]
That Millie would have The Throne

This had all been ratified
Her throne was marked "Reserved"
But Steve, who was near, had a different idea [3]
This being "first come, first served"

Support for Steve was widespread
A woman boss made men wary
How could someone reign with a dizzy brain
And who wasn't big and hairy?

It wasn't known that Millie worked out
With a latest fitness device
She were now quite a size with muscly thighs
That gripped her horse like a vice

Steve had conciliatory leanings
Unlike vengeful Normans before
So when two vassals nicked some castles
He should've – but didn't – wage war

Indeed, no reprisals were taken
So the Barons revolted en masse
It was patently wrong for him not to be strong
He should've kicked some … behind

We were supposedly out of the Dark Ages
But these times were horribly bleak
This man, who meant well, wrought lawless hell
In those days kind equalled weak

Every man Jack for himself
Build your house from brick if you could
Fight for your lives – the strongest survive
Wolves lurked in the wood

Wait up! – Who's that on the Continent?
Lurking in the shadows of night
On a crumpled horse – Why, it's Millie, of course! [4]
Coming to claim her right

She'd become a formidable woman
No one else to match her
No aspects of the weaker sex
Much like Maggie Thatcher!

In a manic act of chivalry
Steve went to meet his aggressor
Then settled her down in Bristol Town
All nice and comfy, bless her! [5]

From there she conquered all about
Rapidly gathering pace
His bad manners before had got stuck in her craw
She'd a mind to punch his face!

They finally fought a Civil War
That lingered on for years [6]
At its end it was deduced that all it produced
Was heartache, blood and tears

Soft Steve came out on top
Remaining as Stephen the First
Because history records that Barons and Lords
Decided that he was least worst [7]

Of all our many Royals
Steve's efforts were notably bad
A man to deplore, cock-ups by the score
He's rated the worst we've had! [8]

Stuff about Stephen

1. Henry was very generous to Stephen giving him much money and land, including Normandy (i)
2. Despite a second marriage (Matilda died in 1118), to Adela of Louvain, only three months after William's death in the White Ship disaster of 1120, no male heir was born and in 1127 he made the barons, including Stephen, swear allegiance to his daughter, The Empress Matilda.(i) (See also "Stuff" about "Henry I")
3. Stephen was crowned on 22nd December 1135, 21 days after Henry's death. He was also recognised as Duke of Normandy, which he was to visit only once, in 1137, and lost to Geoffrey Plantagenet (of Anjou) in 1145 (i)
4. Matilda returned to England in 1139 to claim the Throne. (i)
5. He was also perhaps too chivalrous for his own good and his leniency could be seen as weakness.(i)
6. Civil War continued from Matilda's return until 1153 when, by the Treaty of Winchester, Stephen, partly in return for the promise of lifetime possession of the Throne, recognised Matilda's son (later Henry II) as his heir.(i)
7. The (largely Norman) barons had signed the oath but they claimed its terms allowed Stephen to take the throne (because of Matilda's foreign marriage) and also they could not countenance a female monarch (i) As time wore on their support for Stephen faltered but the continuing civil wars allowed them to take more and more control. (iii)
8. "By general agreement Stephen is considered one of the worst kings the nation has ever had ... out of his depth ... people [at the time] said it was a time when 'Christ and his saints slept'" (ii)

More Stuff about Stephen

(i) Gardiner, Juliet, Ed; The History Today Who's Who in British History; Collins and Brown; London; 2000.
(ii) Hilliam, D; Kings, Queens, Bones and Bastards; Sutton Publishing; Thrupp, Gloucestershire, England; 1999
(iii) Schama, S; A History of Britain (3000 BC – AD 1603); BBC Worldwide Limited; London; 2000.

C. Díaz

HENRY II [1]
Headstrong Henry

(1133 – 1189)
(r.1154 – 1189)

We'll not rue Stephen's parting
He never got a grip
Now to reveal a man of steel
Who'll right the sinking ship

Henry's gentle diplomacy
Had left Steve far from thrilled
He'd said "So long as you're agreed that I'll succeed
I won't have you killed!" [2]

In those bygone, lawless days
Nothing was cast in stone
But Henry was strong and before very long
Sat proudly on The Throne

Henry had lived in Northern France
Le Mans – or quite nearby
Born less in advance and given a chance
He'd have given car racing a try

Like today's ace drivers
Boasting guts and bottle
He augmented his brains; attacked life's chicanes
All that he did was full throttle

Always astute and dynamic
Though a little despotic for some
Being steadfastly resolved many problems were solved
Far better times were to come

He told Barons, who'd been running wild
"In future you'll do my bidding"
Then he burnt their castles and butchered the rascals
To show them he wasn't kidding

Fragmented power was a thing of the past [3]
Royal control the norm
Matters fiscal, of law, and political
All came in for reform

When the Church gave him grief
He made his pal their top man [4] [5]
To have this devotion seemed a very good notion
- But that's when his troubles began

On paper his plan was fool-proof
Surely no one could wreck it
But he hadn't a clue what great power would do
To the turncoat Thomas-à-Becket [6]

"Who'll rid me of this turbulent priest?"
In frustration and anger, he cried
"For, far from a chum this man has become
A ruddy great thorn in my side"

Four boot-licking knights that heard him [7]
Acted tout-suite for their boss
Their plan didn't falter – Tom was stabbed at the altar
Which must have made God pretty cross!

Henry, though stuffed with riches
Was bent on further gain
So he wed a "grey mare" with cash to spare
Eleanor of Aquitaine [8]

Though Henry held power and order
And successes littered his life
He failed in his goal to bring any control
To four errant sons and his wife [9]

His romance with Fair Rosamond [10]
Caused another marital hitch
He didn't half suffer because Ellie was tougher
She could be a right stroppy ... woman

She turned the lads against him
All four took her side
There was no sentiment; they vowed not to relent
Committed to patricide

Four against one looked pretty good odds
And finally Henry lay dead
But it took eighteen years, blood, anguish and tears
And then he died in bed!

Henry made many advances
Especially regarding the law
They single him out – there is no shred of doubt
We've a lot to thank this man for

Stuff about Henry II

1. Henry II was the son of The Empress Matilda (see also Stuff about Stephen and Henry I) and Geoffrey of Anjou; he was named Henry after his maternal grandfather and his mother's first husband. "Plantagenet" comes from his father's chivalric badge of the yellow broom, the Planta Genesta. (ii)

2. In 1153 Stephen, partly in return for the promise of lifetime possession of the Throne, recognized Matilda's son (later Henry II) as his heir.(i) (See also Stephen "Stuff 3")

3. The development of English common law, applied throughout the country, uniformly by the King's courts, and at his direction (i) are a good example of this. (Ed.)

4. (Saint)Thomas (À) Becket (?1120 – 1170), canonized by [Pope] Alexander III in 1173 and declared a traitor by Henry VIII in 1538, (who ordered that he be restyled simply "Bishop Becket" (iv)) had been a good friend of Henry holding various offices and enjoying a very lavish lifestyle. Though Archbishops of Canterbury were traditionally monks Henry went against that when he appointed Becket in 1162, only a day after Beckett had been ordained as a priest. (i)

5. When appointed Chancellor by Henry on his becoming king, Becket was known simply as "Thomas of London" (iii) The reason for the addition of the "À " to give the full name by which he is known (iv) may have, originally, been accidental (v)

6. Once appointed though, he opposed the King at every turn (much to the puzzlement of people at the time and ever since). (i)

7. Three bishops, excommunicated by Becket, complained to the King (who was in Normandy at the time) and four knights, hearing his anger, crossed The Channel and killed Becket on 29th December 1170. (i)

8. Eleanor of Aquitaine (1122 – 1204) was first married to Louis VII of France but, because no sons were born, the marriage was annulled on the grounds of consanguinity in 1152. (I)

9. Four sons (surviving from a total of five, the first, William, Count of Poitiers, died aged 2 (vii)) joined their mother, Eleanor, in revolt against their father Henry II. Henry, the eldest son, known as "The Young King" was actually crowned during his father's lifetime (a not then unheard of practice), to become the anointed ruler but never counted in the succession of the monarchy as he died before his father (viii). He instigated "The Great Revolt" (1173 – 4) and died in 1183. Richard became Richard I and was succeeded by his brother John, as John I in 1199. The third eldest, Geoffrey, was "in the thick of every family quarrel" and was conspiring with King Phillip II of France but he [Geoffrey] had been killed in a tournament at Paris in 1186) (i)

10. Henry had a long term relationship with Rosamund (Rose of the World) Clifford. (iv)

More Stuff about Henry II

(i)   Gardiner, Juliet, Ed; The History Today Who's Who in British History; Collins and Brown; London; 2000.

(ii) Schama, S ;A History of Britain (3000 BC – AD 1603); BBC Worldwide Limited; London; 2000;

(iii) http://www.newadvent.org/cathen/14676a.htm

(iv) Various Eds.; The Concise Dictionary of National Biography; Softback Preview by arrangement with Oxford University Press; Great Britain; 1995

(v)   http://en.wikipedia.org/wiki/Thomas_Becket

(vi) http://www.bbc.co.uk/dna/h2g2/A2654741

(vii) http://en.wikipedia.org/wiki/William%2C_Count_of_Poitiers

(viii)http://en.wikipedia.org/wiki/Henry_the_Young_King

RICHARD I
Coeur de Lion –
The Lionheart

(1157 – 1199)
(r.1189 – 1199)

When Headstrong Henry departed
Four strapping sons he'd bred [1]
Two were long gone; whereupon
Dick was the oldest, not dead

It's sad to shatter illusions
But scholar I fear I must
You'll expect a tale of a red blooded male
Well, he was – but only just!

There was a cosmetic marriage [2]
So he'd have a nice ring
But we hear that this ruler – who fancied the jeweller
Was more of a queen than a King [3]

Dick was an Angivan, French to the core [4]
Wholly unversed in our ways
A gay cavalier who never lived here
Well – six months in all his days

As for a character reference
Call me a romantic fool
But can it be right that a chivalrous knight
Was wicked, vengeful and cruel?

These words fitted Dick like a glove
Though it can't be denied he was brave
Right from the start he'd had a cold heart
And hounded his dad to his grave [5]

But one thing he did for his father
To honour a pledge he'd made
To make a stand in The Holy Land
And fight The Third Crusade

Dick was ready in Eleven Ninety
With a fearsome army and fleet
To a man, fearless fighters and big ugly blighters
Who were expected to win by a street!

(Did Robin Hood go with Dick
To fight with verve and vim?
You might well feel that as he wasn't real [6]
The chances are quite slim!)

On route were Sicily and Cyprus [7]
So he naturally conquered the pair
By this coup he'd outdone the marauding Hun
Who'd also planned to go there

(That's why now it's a German's instinct
To prove they're nobody's fool
They're up with the lark and quick off the mark
To get their place by the pool!)

The Holy Land games started well
With wins at Acra and Joppa
But they took their toll and faced with their goal [8]
Dick and his men came a cropper

Jerusalem held firm
With courage, guile and zeal
The mighty Saladin had thwarted Dick's win [9]
Time to strike a deal!

A blood-sparing treaty was signed
Dick had won some rights
The result, I recall, was that Christians all
Could visit their holy sites

An ill wind sunk Dick's ship
When barely half way home
He saved his skin but was taken in,
Prisoner of Henry of Rome [10]

A ransom involved pots of money
And fiefdom for all his land
This meant that Dick had to get there quick
If Henry needed a hand

For the last five years of Dick's life
War with France was his quest
With never a thought of cutting it short
War's what he liked, and did best

At just forty two years of age
An arrow and he had a meeting [11]
It struck to his core and with one final roar
The lion's heart stopped beating

Stuff about Richard I

1. See Henry II "Stuff 9".
2. This was the marriage, in Limassol en route to a Crusade in 1191, to Berengaria, daughter of Sancho VI of Navarre, which ensured the safety of Richard's southern dominions. (i)
3. His homosexuality was a 20th Century addition to the many legends about Richard (see also "Robin Hood" below). (i)
4. Angevin Empire is "a term invented by historians to refer to the dominions held by …The Plantagenets (see Henry II Stuff 1) … [when] they ruled England. Included are Normandy, Aquitaine, Anjou, Maine, Touraine. (i)
5. See Henry II "Stuff 9".
6. The association with Robin Hood is attributed to a 16th Century legend. (i)
7. His marriage (see also "Stuff 2" above) followed his victory over Cyprus. (i)
8. In 1192 Richard negotiated terms with Saladin as described in the verses which follow. (passim)
9. Saladin was Sultan of Egypt and Henry II had imposed the "Saladin Tithe" to support early Crusades. (ii)
10. Richard was seized on his way home from the Crusades and held to ransom by Leopold of Austria in conjunction with the Pope, who, in reply to Richard's mother Eleanor, said he could do little to help. Four months later he was handed over to Henry VI, Holy Roman Emperor.(ii)
11. Richard was killed at Castle Chalus (near Limoges) while trying to re-take castles seized by his former ally, Phillip of France. (ii)

More Stuff about Richard I

(i)   Gardiner, Juliet and Wenborn, N, Eds; The History Today Companion to British History; Collins and Brown; London; 1995.

(ii) Schama, S; A History of Britain (3000 BC – AD 1603); BBC Worldwide Limited; London; 2000;

KING JOHN
Lackland

(1166 – 1216)
(r.1199 – 1216)

Next in line, however inept
Has to take command
When Dick had gone it was his brother John
Widely called "Lackland" [1]

A Prince without land – disgraceful!
It wasn't enough to have money
And to highlight his shame with that ruddy nickname
Was that supposed to be funny?

His dad, who knew he was livid
Wanted to prove he was fair
So he sent him awhile to rule the Emerald Isle [2]
And make youthful mistakes over there

John, most surely obliged!
On a scale of political craft
He was way past feckless – much more than reckless
Often as not, plain daft! [3]

Isabel became his first wife [4]
Though she knew it would cost her
She fulfilled his needs 'cos she came with the deeds
To a small allotment – called Gloucester

Before brother Dick went Crusading
He'd a problem not to be ducked
He knew John lusted and couldn't be trusted
Further than he could be chucked

So he told him "Stay in France!
'Cos I've had a bright idea,
Now mind what I say, when I'm away
You're not to set foot over here"

"What's in it for me?" sneered John
"Land" countered Dick, "What you've craved!
An enormous extent on the continent
I'll even have some of it paved"

John agreed, but then reneged
On learning Dick's grand design
Arthur, his nephew, had jumped the queue
Chosen as first in line

John arrived at the double
His authority eager to stamp
But failure beckoned as he came a poor second
To Chancellor, William Longchamp [5]

When Dick had finished crusading
And bought his way out of jail
Young Arthur became a lost pawn in the game
John, it was, who'd prevail

His reign was fraught with problems
Beginning with French King Phil
They'd been good mates on earlier dates [6]
Now John was a bitter pill

He'd schemed to gain French land
And behaved like a dog in a manger
He trod on Phil's toes and got up his nose
The man was in physical danger!

John swapped his wife for another
Whose name was a perfect match [7]
By this alliance he planned to gain more land
With John, there was always a catch!

King Phillip then spied weakness
And didn't hang about
Convinced that he ought to rule south of the water
Made short work of kicking John out [8]

At home more trouble was brewing
To which John had to attend
But from every side they sought to tan his hide
He barely had a friend

After years of his awful behaviour
Of treachery, cruelty and more [9]
The Barons were set to repay the debt
And give the tyrant what for

In the Civil War that followed
John was forced to concede
And to supplicate and learn his fate
Over a glass of runny mead [10]

The Barons had made some notes
To reject them – a total non-starter
Now grossly maligned John ceded and signed
The famous Magna Carta [11]

Then they all lived on in peace?
Get real, you hopeless romantic!
John's double dealing increased ill feeling
And the war became more frantic [12]

In the midst of all this mayhem
With so many factions involved
John passed away – it's true to say
That was the main problem solved

Stuff about John

1. He had gained the nickname in his own lifetime, certainly by 1185, but after gaining land, one way or another, and after numerous defeats in battle later became known as "Softsword". (i)
2. He was made Lord of Ireland ("The Emerald Isle") by his father Henry II. (i)
3. When he went to Ireland in 1185 he succeeded in alienating not only the English colonists but also the Irish kings. (i)
4. Betrothed to her by his father he married her in 1189 against the will of The Archbishop of Canterbury but on the orders of King Richard I. John divorced her on becoming king in 1199. (i)
5. William Longchamp was Richard's First Minister and John rebelled against him in 1193 on hearing of Richard's imprisonment. (i)
6. Although "Phil" (Phillip II of France) was once an ally, of John (who had given him Eastern Normandy to gain military support) he was a bitter enemy of John's brother, Richard. Phillip went to war with John when John was trying to regain Richard's support. (i)
7. John married Isabella of Angoulême in 1200 despite her betrothal to Hugh of Lusignan (whose son she married in 1218). (i)
8. Phillip (partly persuaded to action by Hugh of Lusignan (see "Stuff 6") eventually disposed John of his French lands. (ii) (There goes the rest of Normandy! (Ed.)
9. John never trusted anyone, let alone the Barons, and rather than earn their support, as his father had done, through reward and favouritism, John used any means, extortion included, to guarantee loyalty and ended up effectively guaranteeing disloyalty. (iii)
10. Magna Carta, instigated by the barons who were inspired by the defeat of John's army (he himself was not present and few people felt the need to support the man who had, it was, and is, widely believed, murdered his nephew Arthur) at Bouvines in 1214 by Phillip (see stuff 5) was signed at Runnymeade in 1215. (iii)
11. Signed by John to placate the Barons was not "the birth certificate of freedom but the death certificate of despotism" (iii). (Ed.)
12. It was only months before the peace of the charter broke down and the Barons offered the throne of England to Philip of France's son (later Louis VIII) who arrived in England and did not leave until after John's death and defeats in 1217. (iv)

More Stuff about John

(i)   Gardiner, Juliet, Ed; The History Today Who's Who in British History; Collins and Brown; London; 2000.

(ii)   http://en.wikipedia.org/wiki/Philip_II_of_France

(iii) Schama, S ;A History of Britain (3000 BC – AD 1603); BBC Worldwide Limited; London; 2000;

(iv) Gardiner, Juliet and Wenborn, N, Eds; The History Today Companion to British History; Collins and Brown; London; 1995.

Henry III
"Hopeless Henry"

(1207 – 1272)
(r.1216 – 1272)

There he is down in the courtyard
Over by the castle gates
With a paper crown and socks rolled down
Playing footie with his mates [1]

Wait! – An aide's approaching
He brings news hard and cruel
And he heartlessly said; "It's your father, he's dead.
Now you'll have to rule"

"But all you have left is The Midlands,
And the sharp bit in the South West
The French have fleeced London and the East
The barons have conquered the rest [2]

"You're looking bewildered young man
I'll explain as best I can
You've your dad to thank – frankly, he stank
England's gone right down the pan"

"Thank you Job" said Henry
"My dad being dead is -- a shame
I'd take a firm line but I'm only just nine
So I'd rather get back to my game!"

It was propitious that there was a man
To whom the barons were partial
As Henry's first Regent he seemed heaven sent
His name was "William the Marshal" [3]

When Will and the barons joined forces
The French were destined to cop it
And in due course the incumbents were forced
To get on their frogs' legs and hop it [4]

When William's life had ended
Hugh de Burgh kept the country alive [5]
And nice and steady, 'til Henry felt ready
By then he was twenty-five [6]

Still his arrogance knew no bounds
Political skills were none
By twelve fifty-eight it was all too late
Hopes of concord were gone

The final straw was more taxes
His onerous debts to pay
The Barons knew he was deep in a stew
And called in to have their say

Backed against the wall
He gave his crooked word
The Provisions of Oxford let him do as he would [7]
Provided their council concurred

Sometimes things don't work out
An equation of obtuse angles
Added up to derision and bitter division
And a multiplication of wrangles

Henry cocked a snook at "Provisions"
Which started a civil war
The battles were fought against Simon de Montfort [8]
Who was his brother-in-law!

Son Edward led "Dad's Army"
They turned out a hopeless shower!
Henry wasn't too thrilled when most got killed
Now Simon held absolute power

Henry and Ed, both captured
Stewed for a year in a cell [9]
De Montfort was smart and had a good heart
So things were shaping up well

Edward, though, made his escape
His gaolers notably slack
When they fought again – Simon was slain [10]
Henry it seemed – was back!

Up he climbed on the throne
Determined to fulfil his rôle
But haplessness and a lifetime's stress
Had taken their full toll

An overall appraisal?
A hopeless so-and-so!
Few rued the day that he passed away
Stand up Ed – Your go!

Stuff about Henry III

1. As can be seen from his dates he was only 9 years old when he became King. (Ed.)
2. The Kingdom had been "torn apart" by the wars and a civil war provoked by his father's (John) mis-rule. (i)
3. Actually "William Marshall" (a layman, son of a minor baron, b. c.1147 d. 1219, and Regent from 1216) but "Guillaume le Maréchal" in an epic poem of the day (French being the polite language of the aristocracy) (iii)
4. William rode into battle aged 70 in 1217 defeating the French at Lincoln. (i)
5. His full name was "Hubert" who had long held high offices of military and administrative significance under John. (ii)
6. As the most influential figure in Henry III's government he effectively controlled the country until Henry reached 25 years old in 1232 when Henry actually imprisoned Hugh (influenced by a rival of Hugh) until they were reconciled, in 1232, but Hugh's powers not restored. (ii)
7. These were in effect another Bill of Rights by which the Barons demanded an end to the King's autocracy. Interestingly, for the time, they were written not only in the usual Latin and French, but Middle English were too. (iii)
8. Simon de Montfort (1208 – 1265) sought to remove many of the King's powers and was the prime opponent of Henry (ii)
9. They were captured by de Montfort after the Battle of Lewes in 1264 (ii)
10. He was killed by Henry's army under Edward (to become Edward I) at Evesham in 1265 and his body dismembered: the chivalry of the previous two centuries of English warfare had gone. (ii)

More Stuff about Henry III

(i)   Gardiner, Juliet and Wenborn, N, Eds; The History Today Companion to British History; Collins and Brown; London; 1995.

(ii) (ii) Gardiner, Juliet, Ed; The History Today Who's Who in British History; Collins and Brown; London; 2000.

(iii) Schama, S; A History of Britain (3000 BC – AD 1603); BBC Worldwide Limited; London; 2000

(iv) "http://en.wikipedia.org/wiki/William_Marshal,_1st_Earl_of_Pembro ke accessed 2nd January 2015"

C. Díaz

EDWARD I
Longshanks ¹

(1272 – 1307)
(r. 1272 – 1307)

Looking down on his firstborn cherub
And thinking how lucky he'd got
Henry wondered why the little chap's tootsies ²
Stuck out from the end of his cot

The head Royal Chippy was called for
And asked for a verbal report
On why his joiners had gone and cut corners
And made the cot two feet too short

"With utmost respect" said the tradesman
"I'm sure I haven't gone wrong
I've just had a peek, your baby's a freak
His back and his legs are too long!"

He perhaps could have worded that better
Henry's face turned florid red
Then he got the shmuck to carve a new block
On which he removed his fat head

The fact is that Ed was massive
Imposing, and handsome to boot
That's why he'd the nickname "Longshanks"
(A shank's from your knee to your foot)

At fifteen, when he got married
To Eleanor of Castille ³
They got presents of vassals, Earldoms and castles
A household, Chancery and Seal ⁴

The seal was his prize possession
A big one was worth a few groats
His could balance balls and make honking calls
Whilst guarding one of his moats

At sixteen, impatient and angry
A trouble to keep on the rails
Fearless of harm he raised his own army
But lost to Llewelyn in Wales [5]

Ignominious defeat was the outcome
Not good for a future King
So Simon de Montfort lent him support [6]
The lad was under his wing

Simon, (his uncle) the wily old fox
Knew exactly what he was doing
He'd manoeuvred the lad against his dad
In the Civil War that was brewing

But his foul plan was undone
Father and son found accord
Ed fought for the Crown and put the uprising down
De Montfort died by Ed's sword

Kingship really changed Edward
Violent, wild ways hit the dust
In contrast, quite tame, he duly became
Efficient, patient and just

Eleanor grew fifteen branches [7]
To sprout off Ed's family tree
When she'd gone he wed French Margaret instead [8]
She chipped in with three

Ed finally harpooned Wales
Which had always been his wish
But convincing a Scot to throw in his lot
– That's a far different kettle of fish!

"The Hammer of the Scots" [9]
He'd remorselessly attack
But although he was feared, and lines appeared
This nut was a devil to crack

During one particular pillage
Whilst looking for things to nick
He took a stone from a place called "Scone" [10]
A very important brick!

Willie Wallace who lead the resistance [11]
(Or so the story's told)
Devised a way at each fearful affray
To make English blood run cold

A saltire on his face
Plus unkempt and hairy
With these employed he looked annoyed
Murderous and scary

Victory over The Braveheart [12]
Would bring no lasting truce
The Scots held their ground and they rallied around
The courageous Robert the Bruce [13]

Marching north to meet his rival
Ed took shelter from rain
Not far from Carlisle he lay down for a while
Never to rise again.

Stuff about Edward I

1. He was tall even by today's standards but in his time stood head and shoulders above other men; when his tomb in Westminster Abbey was opened in 1774 he was found to be 6 feet 2 inches (about 1.88m). (i) (See also Verse 5)

2. Edward's father was Henry III "who loved quiet as well as peace". (i)

3. Eleanor of Castille (1242 – 1290) was Edward's constant companion since their marriage (in 1254 when he was Prince of Wales). She even accompanied him on Crusades (1270 – 1272 and 1287 – 1291 [when Acre fell]). She died in Nottinghamshire and Edward had an "Eleanor Cross" erected at each of the stopping places of the cortège on its way back to London: the last was Charing Cross. (i)

4. The Great Seal of England was kept in Chancery, but as the king travelled about the country he used a "privy" seal (originally a "private" or "personal" seal, later replaced by a "signet" kept by his Secretary). The Privy Seal was held by the Keeper of the Privy Seal who became an important Officer of State.(ii)

5. "Llewelyn ap Grufudd (c. 1228 – 1282) (Llewelyn the Last [Prince of Wales]). His death in battle brought about the final demise of any Welsh hopes for a Principality. He was also known in Welsh as "Our Last Leader". (v)

6. Edward, while fighting with his father's side, was defeated by Simon at the Battle of Lewes in 1264, but escaped and beat him at Evesham next year. (i) (See also poem "Henry III")

7. Sources vary slightly as to just how many (legitimate) children Edward had by his two wives; but it is certainly around 18. (Ed.) The last of Eleanor's (15?) children became Edward II (1284 – 1327). (i)

8. Edward married Margaret of France (1282 – 1318) in 1299 and, as half-sister of Phillip IV of France she played the rôle of peacemaker between her husband, then after her death, her stepson Edward II, and France. (i)

9. Edward massed the biggest army seen until the 17th Century when he went to war with the Scots and this soubriquet was inscribed on his Westminster tomb in the 16th Century. (i)

10. In one of his Scottish campaigns Edward captured Berwick (then Scotland's largest town) carrying off not only the Scottish Crown Jewels but also the Stone [used as a seat] of Scone (there are several names, including "The Stone of Destiny") on which Scottish Kings had been enthroned. He believed it gave him the right to the Scottish Throne. It has been under the Coronation Chair in Westminster ever since although rumours have it that it has been returned to Scotland and the Westminster Stone is a replica.(i) & (iv)

11. William Wallace (died 1305) was a soldier who slaughtered Edward's army at Stirling Bridge in 1297 but in 1298 was beaten at Falkirk by

superior archers and cavalry. He fought on (in relative obscurity) but was eventually betrayed, captured, and executed at Smithfield in London.(i)

12. This name for Wallace lives on inspiring Scottish patriotism (Nationalism? [Ed.]) to this day. A "Blockbuster" film of that name was made in 1995.(iii)

13. In 1306 Robert Bruce (1274 – 1329) murdered John Comyn, a leading Scottish baron close in line of succession in Scotland, and took the Scottish Throne (becoming Robert I of Scotland). Battles and changing fortunes, including long periods in hiding, ensued until recognition by Edward II in 1328. (i)

More Stuff about Edward I

(i) Gardiner, Juliet, Ed; The History Today Who's Who in British History; Collins and Brown; London; 2000.

(ii) Gardiner, Juliet and Wenborn, N, Eds; The History Today Companion to British History; Collins and Brown; London; 1995.

(iii) Wallace, R, writer; Gibson, M., director; Braveheart; Feature film; TCF/Icon/Ladd; USA; 1995.

(iv) http://www.highlanderweb.co.uk/wallace/destiny.htm

(v) http://en.wikipedia.org/wiki/Llywelyn_ap_Gruffudd#Last_campaign_and_death

C. Diaz

EDWARD II
T'other way Ted

(1284 – 1327)
(r. 1307-1327)

Ted being King was a long shot
It's strange how life unfurls
As it came to pass older siblings en masse
Were dead – or even worse – girls! [1]

Some destinies fit the bill
Others, you'd rather swop
This twist of fate was not so great
Ted was a miserable flop!

His father, away at the Wars
Too busy to get to the 'phones
Had failed to detect the young man's defect
A surfeit of female hormones [2]

At sixteen his path was chosen
Or so the stories allege
When a Gascon called Piers and some other young men [3]
Tipped the lad over the edge

He certainly didn't like fighting
And soldiering? –He hadn't a clue!
So the Scottish war as was fashioned before [4]
Was last thing he wanted to do

"Just my luck" he whimpered
"Dad's left me with this struggle
All those big strapping Jocks in tartan frocks
And not one who'll give me a cuddle!"

With The Bruce at the peak of his power
Ted's troops had to adjourn
They couldn't cope and gave up hope
When they lost at Bannockburn [5]

The conflict that Longshanks had started
Plagued his feeble heir
And the unification of the British Nation
Became a total nightmare

Ted married and had four kiddies
Despite his leanings in bed
Fortuitously then, for the succession
His pencil had plenty of lead

He'd quickly defamed his father
Causing discontentment untold
This dopey kid changed all his dad did
Before he'd a chance to go cold

All of the Barons were enraged!
They despised this delinquent buffoon
And the way he'd scheme to favour his "harem"
Went down like a lead balloon

Piers, who's previously mentioned
Ted's foremost libertine
Was vested impearl and created an Earl
And postured like his Queen

The Barons hated Piers
For his arrogance, cheek and vice
He mocked the Crown so they hunted him down
And he paid the final price [6]

Piers replacement didn't fare better
Hugh Despenser was he [7]
If you don't like gory avoid this story
Went to the dogs – literally!

Ted's wife, meanwhile, who'd left him
(Hardly a great surprise)
Went on the run with an exiled Baron
To plot the King's demise [8]

Their coup worked like a charm
Dynamic, short and sweet
With few on Ted's side and his defences rent wide
They'd not a fat lot to beat

Locked up in a cold, dark dungeon
(He'd not been there too long)
Ted was heard to curse; "Things can't get worse"
Not for the first time – wrong!

His murder in twenty-seven [9]
Completed his fall from grace
A lone funeral bell tolled a sad death knell
For a total waste of space

Stuff about Edward II

1. Edward I "probably had 17 children" by his two wives Eleanor of Castile and Margaret of France. (i)
2. Most sources refer to Edward's (probable) homosexuality (Ed.)
3. Piers Gaveston, son of a Gascon noble in Edward I's service *, was an early favourite of Edward, even before his ascension as Edward II. This had been noticed, for example, by Isabella of France, then aged 12, arriving to marry Edward in 1305, when Gaveston was wearing jewellery given to Edward by Isabella's father. (ii)
4. Edward I had left his son with a war against "... a formidable enemy, Robert Bruce [of Scotland] ..." (iii)
5. The Scots were outnumbered 3 to 1 at Bannockburn in 1314 but Robert the Bruce chose to fight on wet ground which did not favour the heavily equipped army of Edward. Edward was defeated and 4000 "... English, Welsh, Gascon and Scots enemies of the Bruces..." were killed..." (iv)
6. Gaveston was murdered in 1312 (i) (See also "Stuff 3")
7. Hugh Despenser and his father were both courtiers and the son (and possibly the father too (ii)) became Edward's favourite. (i)
8. The invasion by Isabella of France and Mortimer (Roger Mortimer, 1st Earl of March, earlier a good ally of Edward, but changed after the excesses of the new favourite, Despenser) met little opposition and led to the execution of both Despensers and Edward's imprisonment and abdication in favour of his son Edward III. (i)
9. It was said he died in prison, probably murdered in a "most gruesome fashion". (i)

More Stuff about Edward II

(i) Gardiner, Juliet and Wenborn, N, Eds; The History Today Companion to British History; Collins and Brown; London; 1995.
(ii) Hilliam, David; Kings, Queens, Bones and Bastards; Sutton Publishing Limited; Stroud, Gloucestershire, England; 1998.
(iii) Gardiner, Juliet, Ed; The History Today Who's Who in British History; Collins and Brown; London; 2000.
(iv) Schama, S; A History of Britain (300 B.C. – A.D. 1603); BBC Worldwide; London; 2000

C. Diaz

EDWARD III
"War Ed"

(1312 – 1377)
(r. 1327 –1377)

Ed told Isabella, his mother
"I'm keen to get a-head"
So she went and got his father's
And stuck it on the end of his bed [1]

Ed's father ("T'other way Ted")
Had run the country down
And power mad Izzy had long been busy
Preparing young Ed for the Crown

"But you're not ready yet" she told him
"You're still only a pup
So I'll hold the fort with my boyfriend Mort [2]
Just 'til your acne clears up"

Roger Mortimer, the afore mentioned lover
Craved power and was well chuffed
So, when Ed was full grown and wanted his throne
Rog told him to go and get ... lost"

No way was Ed having that!
And plotted an insurrection
He demanded command and could not understand
Why he needed a perfect complexion

He won and took resolute action
Even though he was young
Because they'd up-risen his mum went to prison
And Rog was highly strung [3]

Ed got wed whilst only sixteen [4]
And nature took its course
He wanted a throng who'd grow big and strong
To be his driving force

In this he achieved great success
Five boys lived 'til their prime
A useful quintet as he'd often forget
And start several wars at a time

Unlike his androgynous father
Ed was pure masculine
Follow a trail of death and travail
That's how you'd know where he'd been

So keen was he on battle
This English conquistador
That his kingdom and time to come
Is known as "The Hundred Years War" 5

Disputes over land and power
Mistrust and deep discord
Under each stone a contentious bone
Decided by the sword

One conflict bled into another
The stakes were always high
Endless brawls with the pesky Gauls
Rarely knowing why!

Often to keep men busy
Or to give his subjects a treat
A gory story of death and glory
Had them dancing in the street 6

Good health, it's true to say
Was in very short supply
Pestilence, The Ague and Bubonic Plague
Countless folk would die! 7

A Chamber was added to Parliament
It needed to be overhauled
A second house for people with nous
But what should it be called?

They chose the name 'The Commons" 8
And to this day that's stuck
Fitting, as the average MP does tend to be
Nowadays common as muck!

Ed's conduct when his wife passed away
Was respectful and polite
He'd didn't make a pass at another lass
'Til her hearse was well out of sight

Then Alice Perrers came along [9]
The lady to whom he'd succumb
She became his crutch and he couldn't see much
From his station, under her thumb

Alice made all the decisions
Whether he liked it or no
Now way past his prime – he'd had his time
The man had got to go!

So, how shall we mark his paper?
To judge how his fifty years went
Ticks and crosses for gains and losses
A touch under fifty percent! [10]

Stuff about Edward III

1. All sources refer to Isabella's suspected involvement in the murder of Edward II, her estranged husband. (Ed.)
2. Most sources refer to Edward II's (probable) homosexuality and Isabella, his wife, took a lover, Roger Mortimer. (Ed.) Mortimer had been imprisoned by Edward II but escaped from the Tower and went to France where he met Isabella. (i)
3. Resolute indeed, he had both mother and her lover arrested, and Mortimer was hanged and Isabella spent the next 31 years under house arrest until her death in 1358. (ii)
4. In 1328 Edward married Philippa of Hainault (Flanders, not London [and certainly not the Central Line (Ed.)]) who later encouraged the wealth-bringing wool trade with Flanders. (ii)
5. "The Hundred Years War", a term coined in the 19th Century, was with France and related to the English claims to territory in France, continued intermittently (for example, there was a truce from 1396 to 1424) until final French victory (at Castillon) in 1453. (i)
6. It may seem strange but people often welcomed war; the King (not just Edward) because it kept people's minds off home events, and the people because it provided employment and something to cheer about (at least in victory). (Ed.)
7. "The Black Death" (so called since the 18th Century) arrived through Dorset ports in 1348 and within 18 months spread throughout Britain; it is estimated that England lost about 2 million of its population of about 6 million with attendant economic disaster throughout Europe. (i)
8. The name came about at that time when a "Commons Clerk" was appointed. (i)
9. A royal mistress whose increasing influence after Queen Philippa's death in 1369 brought with it blame for some of the problems of the last years of Edwards reign as he became senile. (i)
10. Although his reign saw military victories and peace at home the wars were extremely expensive and some historians, at least until the end of the 20th Century felt Edward was to blame for some of the monarchy's later instability. (i)

More Stuff about Edward III

(i)   Gardiner, Juliet and Wenborn, N, Eds; The History Today Companion to British History; Collins and Brown; London; 1995.
(ii) Hilliam, David; Kings, Queens, Bones and Bastards; Sutton Publishing Limited; Stroud, Gloucestershire, England; 1998.

C. Diaz

70

RICHARD II
"Tricky Dicky"

(1367 – 1400)
(r. 1377 –1399)

Young Dicky had a visit
From his Majesty's head consort [1]
He had not, in truth, to be a sleuth
To tell the man was fraught

He was hopping from foot to foot
In a manic sort of jig
His clothes out of place, a daft looking face
And was sweating like a pig

He said; "I've been to see your grandpa
He's on his bed, outspread
And, truth to tell he's not too well
In fact, the blighter's dead!"

"Now, your dad should take over [2]
Of that there's little doubt
But, you may recall, he's dead and all [3]
Which, sort of, rules him out

So according to my records
Which I'm sure are up to date
The kingly crown has been passed down
And landed on your plate"

"If you're pulling my leg" said Dicky;
"I'll have you strung up by the thumbs.
Now don't make me laugh, I'm ten and a half
And can't even do my sums!"

But kingship was his destiny
And in order to survive
And he was duly taught sums of the sort:
How many beans make five

A council ruled whilst he grew
Uncle John Gaunt in the chair [4]
In The Plague's awful wake there was much heartache
And a dour, cheerless air

When Dick, aged just fourteen
Raised tax for his Royal Purse [5]
Very far from halt "The Peasants Revolt" [6]
Things went from bad to worse

You've probably heard of Wat Tyler [7]
Who in this cause was engrossed
A belligerent sort, who it's fair to report
Was more revolting than most

Dick's first wife, Bohemia Anne [8]
Was a cracker, by repute
But despite many tries her early demise
Came prior to her 'bearing fruit'

Isabella was wife number two [9]
Une accorde très politic
A wicked comport to our way of thought
This match seemed horribly sick

If God had got wind of their union
He'd never have let him in heaven
As he, at the time, was aged twenty-nine
And Izzy was only just seven!

When Gaunt John duly passed on [10]
Dicky nicked his loot
Henry, John's lad, was hopping mad
And rancorous to boot

Dick's supporters were routed [11]
Some of them had to die
This was clearly no blip so the rest jumped ship
Dicky was left high and dry

Now Henry ascended the Throne
To barely diluted acclaim
And as the last Henry, you see, had been number three
Stuck a four after his name

Meanwhile in a castle dungeon
Dick knew he'd lost the fight
Quite devoid of a friend, at his tunnel's end
Barely a flicker of light

Dick's suffering wasn't to last
Thus came the final coup
When Henry's mates who were passing the gates
Popped in to run him through [12]

Too many dicky decisions
Ill advised and unfair
Always listen to your tuition
And count your beans with care!

Stuff about Richard II

1. The "Majesty" here referred to being Edward III (Ed.)
2. Richard II's father was Edward III's son, Edward, The Black Prince (who gained that name for reasons now unknown) who in the 16th Century had been "one of the outstanding English leaders in the Hundred Years War" (see also "Stuff 6" to Edward III). (ii)
3. The Black Prince died in 1376 of an illness arising from the dysentery he had contracted 10 years earlier. (ii)
4. John of Gaunt (1340 – 1399) was born in Ghent (hence "Gaunt") and was a younger son of Edward III. He had much land and was immensely wealthy; he was loyal to the Crown even exiling his own son (Bolingbroke, later Henry IV) at Richard's behest. (ii)
5. Richard II was largely not held to blame for events so early in his life, much of that blame falling on his advisor John of Gaunt (see also "Stuff 4" above) whose Savoy palace was burned down, but tax increases did not help the situation. (ii)
6. In June 1381 rebellion, known as the Peasant's Revolt occurred when attempts were made to collect a Poll Tax, the last in a long line of injustices. (i)
7. Wat Tyler, a hitherto unknown, and still largely unidentified, peasant, was famous for a week as a leader of the revolt but died after a scuffle with the King's men at a meeting in June 1381. After that the rebellion soon collapsed and Richard, with Parliament's connivance reneged on the promises he had made to the peasants. (i)
8. Anne of Bohemia (1367 – 1394) was sister of King Wenceslas of Bohemia and married Richard II in 1382. He was inconsolable on her death, ordering the destruction of Sheen, the manor house in Surrey in which she died. (ii)
9. Isabella of France [there have been several Isabella's of France – Ed.] (1389 – 1409) married Richard in 1396 (see subsequent verse) but returned to France after Richard had been deposed (see subsequent verses and below) where she re-married (Charles of Orléans), dying in child birth while still not yet 20. (ii)
10. When John of Gaunt died in 1399 Richard was "... a very wealthy king but went nowhere without an armed guard ..." and had dispossessed a third of the upper nobility. (ii)
11. Bolingbroke, who would be Henry IV, met no real resistance and Richard was forced to abdicate in 1399. (ii)
12. There was in fact a plot to rescue Richard but its failure prompted Henry to have him murdered. (ii)

More Stuff about Richard II

(i) Gardiner, Juliet and Wenborn, N, Eds; The History Today Companion to British History; Collins and Brown; London; 1995.
(ii) Gardiner, Juliet, Ed; The History Today Who's Who in British History; Collins and Brown; London; 2000.

HENRY IV
Bolingbroke [1]

(1366 – 1413)
(r. 1399 – 1413)

The reign of Tricky Dicky [2]
Was an unmitigated disaster
It marked the decline of The Angevin Line [3]
Now for The House of Lancaster

Henry, Tricky's cousin
Had set his heart on being king
Henry Bolingbroke!!.... You'd expect a joke
That must be a very sore thing!

An onerous task lay ahead
A country in disarray
A nice new broom could lift the gloom
And sweep the troubles away?

So, did he hit the bulls-eye?
No! As history does recall
It's sad to record that he missed the board
And the surrounding wall!

Was destiny in his hands though?
Did he ever stand a chance?
It seems he was struck by wretched luck
A victim of circumstance!

In the north, the Scots as usual
Endlessly struggling for power
Then out to the west the Welsh a pest
Inspired by Owen Glendower [4]

He was a fearsome forward
Who loved a scrummy war
Devoid of fears he'd got cauliflower ears
And was built like a sh– house door

Then, of course, The Frenchies [5]
Always a pain in the rear!
With furious intent on the continent
And the odd sortie over here

Wholesale insurrections
He could neither defeat nor appease
An endless procession of naked aggression
Would bring this king to his knees

On a notable occasion
Whilst lynching some mutineers
He killed Archbishop Scrope, a mate of the Pope [6]
– Not one of his better ideas!

So thumping were his headaches
He thought God was taking the Mick
Or bringing this strife to his wretched life
For murdering Scrope and Dick [7]

His sanctimonious holiness
Made God deaf to his prayers
Kings who aren't in charge and whose foibles are large
Don't impress him upstairs

His first wife, Mary, had virtues and kids
But the second came with a hitch
Joan of Navarre was wholly bizarre
Not to mention a practicing witch! [8]

When asked to explain her antics
He didn't know how to respond
Truth to tell he'd been under her spell
Since she'd stirred his tea with her wand [9]

With a reputation in tatters
His innings drew to a close
Now near and far he was unpopular
Like a spot on the end of your nose

Henry's dotage was ghastly
Quite literally losing face [10]
His skin fell to bits – he began to have fits
So his son Henry V took his place

This verse is thin on facts
And it lacks a plot
Well forsooth – Here's the truth
He achieved diddly squat!

Yet though he did so little
A playwright who's close to our hearts
Got carried away with Henry's resumé
And told his tale in two parts. [11]

Stuff about Henry IV

1. So called after his birthplace, Bolingbroke in Lincolnshire. (ii)
2. Also known as Richard II – see previous poem (Ed.)
3. Angevin Empire is "a term invented by historians to refer to the dominions held by ... The Plantagenets (see Henry II Stuff 1) ... [when] they ruled England. Included are Normandy, Aquitaine, Anjou, Maine, Touraine. (i) (See also "Richard I Stuff 4" (Ed.))
4. Owen Glendower (c. 1355 – c. 1416 [the exact date and place of his death are unknown]) was known in Welsh as "Owain Glen Dwr". He led many a rebellion against the English, from the time of the political unrest after the dethronement of Richard II. Eventually the Welsh were overcome by the English power and wealth to support it. (ii)
5. The French had lent Glendower (see "Stuff 4" above) support. (ii)
6. Archbishop of York Richard Scrope (1350 – 1405) opposed the king and actually joined the "Percy Rebellion" led by Henry Percy ("Hotspur") being executed after an "irregular" trial, and his tomb in York Minster became the centre of a popular cult. (ii)
7. Many believed that the leprosy from which Henry suffered was God's punishment for the murder of His servant Scrope, if not Richard II too. (ii)
8. Joan of Navarre (c. 1373 -1437), was the daughter of the King of Navarre, and married Henry in 1403 when she was the widowed Duchess of Brittany. Although accused of responsibility for attempts on the life of her stepson, Henry V, by sorcery and necromancy, she was not tried but held in custody until the dying Henry IV had her released after three years. (ii)
9. She must have been a witch then as tea did not come to England until the 1650s. (Ed.)
10. He is believed to have suffered from leprosy (see "Stuff 7" above). (Ed.)
11. Shakespeare's eponymous play has Henry (not the most important character in a play also involving "Hotspur" (see "Stuff 6" above) and Henry V) going from weary but effective (he thinks) in Part I, to tired, ill, and almost tragic in Part II. (iii)

More Stuff about Henry IV

(i)   Gardiner, Juliet and Wenborn, N, Eds; The History Today Companion to British History; Collins and Brown; London; 1995.
(ii) Gardiner, Juliet, Ed; The History Today Who's Who in British History; Collins and Brown; London; 2000. (iii) Boyce, C; Encyclopedia of Shakespeare; Facts on File; New York, NY USA;1990.

HENRY V
"Victory Vee"
Henry of Monmouth [1]

(1387 – 1422)
(r. 1413 – 1422)

"Vee" had studied "One-Vee" carefully
And knew he was unfit
So when the Crown was handed down
He did the opposite [2]

Hard times were dead and gone
A short lived hiatus
Vee was rewarded and duly accorded
His rightful Royal status

Stability, peace and unity
Overdue advance
Which left "Vee" free to cross the sea
To fight for lumps of France

For land that once belonged to us
Frankly, he was jealous
And his rampant pride could not abide
How they had more than us

In the head of this fearless soldier
A masterful military mind
Like he'd pretend to retreat as if he'd been beat
Then creep up from behind!

A stunning battleship was built
Which sailed to wide acclaim
To praise the Lord –and have Him aboard
The Jesus was her name [3]

Frequent tales of battles won
Came from foreign shore [4]
Most outstandingly the victory
He won at Agincourt [5]

October of Fourteen Fifteen
Our history celebrates
That, as fighting goes, if we were the "pro's"
The French were the "under-eights"

They had home advantage
And a lot more men of course
But in the majesty of "Victory Vee"
We had the tour-de-force

Two fingers shown for all to see [6]
Like Churchill would one day
But Henry's 'vee' to France you see
Faced round the other way!

King Charles the Sixth, his rival [7]
(Prepare to be badly misled)
Named it appears for his spaniel-sized ears
Which hung off the side of his head [8]

Charles was bought to heel
And resigned to his fate
Without as much as a moan gave Henry his Throne [9]
And chucked in his daughter, Kate [10]

Talk about coup d'état!
Truly a red-letter day
Now "Vee" would be fine, have loads of nice wine
And a castle in St. Tropez

Dark clouds had brightened
But then to his utter dismay
The silver lining he thought was shining
Turned into a dirty grey

Medical problems were looming
His timer was badly cast
The hole inside was far too wide
His sand was running out fast

His body, once a temple
Couldn't stand any more
Badly healed fusions, cuts and contusions
He succumbed – just thirty-four! [11]

This was not just a consummate soldier
But a man of vision and flair
Hard on the greedy – kind to the needy
A master of firm but fair

Stuff about Henry V

1. Sometimes known as "Henry of Monmouth" after his birthplace. (i)
2. His main lesson was that "... to survive and prosper, a King of England needed to be both messiah and manager ..." (iv)
3. In 1415, the Henry V's English invasion force was carried across the channel by 1500 ships and boats, to fight at Agincourt. Henry V built the Jesus, the first ship of 1000 tons, followed by the Grace Dieu of 1400 tons. (ii)
4. "The dispatches from France were written, and publicized, for the first time, in English..." (iv)
5. The Battle of Agincourt ("Azincourt" in French) took place on 25th October, St. Crispin's Day, when "... the [overconfident] French [having a larger army]...suffered appalling losses at the hands of Henry's archers ..." (v)
6. According to a popular legend the V sign was used by longbow men after winning at Agincourt, the French having earlier said that they would cut off the bowmen's shooting fingers after a French victory. (iii)
7. King Charles VI of France, an "imbecile" in many sources (Ed.) was [from about 1392] "... rarely in his own mind ..." but often called "Well Beloved" by the French at the time. (vi)
8. In fact!... although Spaniels are known to have been in existence at this time The Cavalier King Charles Spaniel was actually named some 200 years later after Charles I of England who kept and adored them as did his successor, Charles II. (Ed.)
9. Charles appointed Henry his heir by The Treaty of Troyes in 1420 after Henry's conquest of Normandy. (i)
10. Henry married Catherine of Valois, daughter of Charles, by the same treaty in 1420 and their son became Henry VI. (i)
11. The day after the marriage Henry set off for more (geographical) conquests in France but died of dysentery in 1422 only a few months before the death of Charles but the English position in France remained "... tenable and profitable for [at least] twenty years." (i)

More Stuff about Henry V

(i)   Gardiner, Juliet, Ed; The History Today Who's Who in British History; Collins and Brown; London; 2000;

(ii)   http://www.royalnavalmuseum.org/info_sheets_naval_history.htm

(iii) http://en.wikipedia.org/wiki/V_sign

(iv) Schama, S; A History of Britain (3000 BC – AD 1603); BBC Worldwide Limited; London; 2000

(v)   http://www.britannia.com/history/narmedhist6.html

(vi) Murray, J; An introductory History of France; Murray; London; (first published 1884, New Edition 1918

C. Diaz

HENRY VI
"Henpecked Henry"

(1421 – 1471)
(r. 1422-1461 and 1470-1471)

Imagine this – You're nine months old [1]
Sucking your favourite teddy
There's jam in your hair and your only care
Is if your "din-din" is ready?

Then a big ugly face invades your space
With an oddly misshapen head
There's a quick "coochy-coo" then with no more ado
He tells you: "Your father's dead!"

How can you know what dead is?
And what does it mean: "been-decreed"?
Now you've to "rule", "oversee" and apparently
Do something called "suck-seed"!

Big rollers cascade from your eyes
You've an uncontrollable chin
And you fix his gaze with a look that says
He's like something the cat's dragged in

"I knew this wouldn't be easy", says he
"As this here meeting confirms
It's plain, for sure, you're a might immature
So I'll put it in layman's terms

A country is like an engine
The King's job – to oil the cogs
You'll have plenty to do because you've to rule two
One full of nasty frogs" [2]

We've taken some interim measures
Two uncles are going to fill in [3]
With these two at the helm we'll steady The Realm
So stop that wobbling chin!"

89

Bedford and Gloucester, this twosome
Drew straws for which country they'd run
Whilst Henry, in the wings, learned Kingly things
Missing out childhood and fun

He bobbed about in the deep end
Barely keeping afloat
His tutor Beauchamp said his brain was "damp" [4]
He was nice – but dull and remote

The French had spawned a hero
Who fought, without fear, for their throne
Just a young lass but a pain in the neck
The Maid of Orleans: Joan! [5]

When she led, the French jumped ahead
What passion she created!
Till the petite brunette proved too much of a threat
And she (and her steak) were cremated

Calais was all we had left
About which it's hard to enthuse
To French regret Brits are there even yet
Now selling fags and cheap booze

Wait! Who's that on the horizon?
It's Margaret of Anjou [6]
This formidable sole is bent on control
A scary and very shrewd shrew

Audacious, ambitious and bumptious
She'd not be circumvented
A rising star who had burned her bra
Before they'd been invented [7]

Her sights were trained on Henry
And soon they tied the knots
Then he got dafter – so what happened thereafter? [8]
Maggie called the shots

The recipe of "Henry Vee"
Had quelled internal trouble
Now sharpened claws opened festering sores
Causing hot blood to bubble

Since Lancastrians got into power [9]
Yorks had out of joint noses
They were livid and so it was their time to blow
This was The War of the Roses [10]

Henry's brain went softer still!
England began to slump
So Richard of York was given his work [11]
Maggie had so got the hump!

This was an Iron Lady
She wasn't about to succumb
But though she fought it all came to nought
Richard's time had come

Henry and Maggie wound up in clink
She still standing tall
But despite a brief escape from this terrible scrape
Their writing was on the wall

Again locked up in the tower
Next day Henry took his last breath
Killed by an assassin who happened to be passing? [12]
Or did Maggie nag him to death!

Stuff about Henry VI

1. Decreed "King" at only 9 months, then, a month later, "King of France" (in accordance with The Treaty of Troyes) on the death of his maternal grandfather, Charles VI (of France). He was declared "of age" in 1437 after which his problems in both kingdoms multiplied. (i)

2. Literally "poetic licence" as it was not known for another month that he would also be King of France (see "Stuff 1". above) (Ed.)

3. One uncle was The First Duke of Bedford, John of Lancaster, who was "Protector" of England during Henry's minority. The second uncle, created "Duke of Gloucester" in 1414, only served as "Protector" during Bedford's absences. (i)

4. In May 1428 a Great Council appointed Richard Beauchamp, Earl of Warwick as governor of the six-year-old Henry VI but he, a soldier, did not get on well with the ascetic, but not meek and mild, Henry and he, Beauchamp, resigned, not to be replaced, in 1436. (ii)

5. Joan of Arc, (Saint Joan, from 1920, one of France's patron saints) was a peasant from Eastern France who asserted that she had visions from God which instructed her to recover her homeland from English. When she fell into English hands in 1431 at the age of 19 she was burnt at the stake. (iii)

6. Margaret of Anjou (1430 – 1482) is often visualised (not the least by William Shakespeare) as a cruel warrior, but, whilst no doubt ambitious and impetuous, also had a love of jewels, whatever the state of the Royal Purse. Her marriage to Henry VI in 1445 was undertaken with the promise of Maine to France. (i)

7. The first modern brassiere to receive a patent was the one invented in 1913 by a New York Socialite named Nary Phelps Jacob. (iv)

8. The Hundred Years War with France finished badly for Henry with the losses of Normandy and Aquitaine and in 1453, after a defeat at Castillon, he suffered a complete breakdown. (i)

9. John of Gaunt, 1340 – 1399, was Duke of Lancaster, as was his son Henry IV. Hence Henry IV, V, and VI, and their families, were known as "Lancastrians". Richard of York, 1411 – 1460, was Duke of York, and his son Edward IV, and then Edward V, Richard III and their families, were known as "Yorkists". (Ed. and various sources)

10. York was represented by a White rose, York by a red. The term "Wars of the Roses" (coined by Walter Scott 18th/19th Century) spread to cover all of the various separate English Civil Wars of the 15th Century (i)

11. Richard of York (1411 – 1460) was appointed "Protector" in 1454 after Henry's breakdown (see "Stuff 8" above). He died in the Battle of Wakefield in 1460 leaving his son as claimant to Henry's throne, which he took, as Edward IV, in 1461. (i)

12. Despite a brief recall (he had fled to Scotland until captured and sent to The Tower in 1465) to the throne in 1470 he was re-imprisoned and murdered (probably on the orders of Edward IV, who saw him as the "last obvious representative of the Lancastrian dynasty") in 1471. (i)

More Stuff about Henry VI

(i)   Gardiner, Juliet, Ed; The History Today Who's Who in British History; Collins and Brown; London; 2000;
(ii) http://yorkistage.blogspot.com/2009/03/richard-beauchamp-and-upbringing-of.html
(iii) http://en.wikipedia.org/wiki/Joan_of_Arc
(iv) http://inventors.about.com/od/bstartinventions/a/brassiere.htm.

C. Díaz

94

EDWARD IV
"Two Times Ted"

(1442 – 1483)
(r.1461 – 70 and 1471- 83)

Hey! What happened to Richard? [1]
Why's he been cast asunder?
He's not around – He's gone to ground
The blighter's six feet under!

Fighting for The Kingdom [2]
He'd almost won the day
When a very sharp spear came dangerously near
The plonker got in its way

His teenage son Ted stepped forward
Will he be up to the task?
He's ready and willing; darned good at killing [3]
What the heck more can you ask?

But he'd to pass a practical
Before they'd call him boss
This challenge was met, without breaking sweat
At The Battle of Mortimer Cross [4]

Elizabeth Woodville won his heart
She, not of Royal blood [5]
The marriage, in fact, was a secret pact
Her name at court was mud!

For Liz had a major drawback
She came from the Red Rose crowd [6]
To a White Rose soul... a complete own goal
That should have been disallowed

But could she deliver babies!
Cripes she could, and no doubt!
All it took was a dirty look
For a bundle of joy to pop out

Ten little cherubs in total
His dutiful partner bore
Ted's distraction with her out of action?
Lovers by the score! [7]

Up steps The Earl of Warwick [8]
And takes an obtuse stance
Left quite unchecked he freed 'Henpecked' [9]
Who jumped at a second chance

So, Henry's back on The Throne
And Warwick's hailed 'Kingmaker' [10]
But not for long because when Ted came back strong [11]
Both needed an undertaker

Ted had learned a hard lesson
No more Mr. Nice Guy
Now cold and terse he showed no mercy
Cross him – and hope to die!

Take his brother, George, for instance
Really quite harshly reproved!
When he and some other guys plotted Teds' demise
Ted had *his* head removed [12]

Here's the juicy part now
An account of Ted's pleasure years
Detailed extracts of sordid facts
This isn't for delicate ears!

[This is a note from the censor
My job's to limit the smut,
Ted was a touch blue but these verses won't do
Five have had to be cut

All you need to know, dear reader
Is Ted had a major fling
Plus, he got lazy and fat, behaved like a … fool
And wasn't a very good king]

But at his Rosy Battles
The pruned rose was Red
'Til one by one their claimants were gone
And Lancastrian hopes lay dead

During Ed's latter years
There's not a lot to report
He was just forty one when God judged he was done
And unplugged his life support [13]

Stuff about Edward IV

1. Edward was the eldest son of Richard of York (1411 – 1460) who had made numerous claims to the throne and was killed during a battle relating to one of those claims, at Wakefield. (i)

2. Actually he was fighting for the Kingship (for himself) rather than for the country (Ed.)

3. He had been involved in his father's battles with the Lancastrians since he was 17 and at 6 feet 3 inches, intelligent, brave and powerfully built, was well equipped for the job. (i)

4. Edward's first victory, in his own right (that is, after his father's death) was at Mortimer's Cross in Hereford in 1461 shortly before he was proclaimed King. (i)

5. Not only was she not "of Royal Blood" (becoming the first commoner to marry an English monarch) she had two sons by her late husband (Sir John Grey, killed at St. Albans in 1461), 5 brothers and 7 unmarred sisters. The King kept the marriage secret for several months clearly foreseeing the trouble it would cause. Indeed, the Woodville family's apparent monopoly of royal patronage upset many including, and particularly, Richard Neville, Earl of Warwick. (i)

6. Elizabeth's first husband was John of Groby, a Lancastrian knight, and her mother's first husband John of Lancaster, third son of Henry IV of England. (ii) (There is far more to this complicated lineage than can be dealt with here. (Ed.)

7. There are many references to Edward's promiscuity and mistress throughout reference works and web sites. (Ed.)

8. See "Stuff 5"

9. Real name "Henry VI" – see also poem 'Henry VI' above.

10. Though once an ally of Edward, Warwick's disaffection with him (see also "Stuff 5" above) led to the switch of his allegiance to the Lancastrian and his part in the (short lived) reinstatement of Henry VI leading in turn to Warwick's nickname "The Kingmaker" (i)

11. Though briefly deposed, in September 1470, Edward regained the throne in 1471 then defeating, and executing, Henry VI. (i)

12. George, Duke of Gloucester, was eventually found guilty of plotting against Edward and was imprisoned in the Tower of London. He was "privately executed" (Shakespearean tradition states he was drowned in a butt of Malmsey wine) on 18th February 1478 (iii)

13. Edward died of natural causes, although some historians say "of illness brought on by his own excesses". (ii)

More Stuff about Edward IV

(i)   Gardiner, Juliet, Ed; The History Today Who's Who in British History; Collins and Brown; London; 2000;

(ii) http://en.wikipedia.org/wiki/John_Grey_of_Groby

(iii) http://en.wikipedia.org/wiki/EdwardIVof_England

EDWARD V
"Tower Ted" [1]

(1470 – [?]1483)
(r.1483)

Some Kings were well adjusted
Others fools and freaks
How would Ted go? – Seems we'll never know
He only lasted eight weeks!

With the passing of "Two Times Ted" [2]
Sadly, cut short in his prime
The first of his breed was meant to succeed
That was the plan at the time

He too was a "Ted" but thirteen and green
Spotty, grotty and rude [3]
Should they employ this difficult boy?
It caused a family feud! [4]

Against the advice of his elders
(This was one stroppy brat!)
He demanded to move to London to prove
He'd look good in his new spiky hat

At his home at Ludlow Castle
(Which he owned being The Earl) [5]
He packed his case and set out to face
The dangers about to unfurl

In the care of an uncle, Earl Rivers [6]
Through forests dark and drear
Life bore no terror – that was an error!
Turned out he had much to fear

An ambush sprang from nowhere
A sneaky little trick!
Ted thought he'd be harmed but quickly felt calmed
It was his uncle, "Dangerous Dick" [7]

What a misguided young fool!
Dick wasn't there as his friend
Awash with loathing this wolf in sheep's clothing
Was the prelude to his end.

"You've a nice comfy room in The Tower", lied Dick
"With charming views, because it's high
I'll sort out the damp, get you a lamp
And a wide screen TV, with Sky" [8]

There was no view, nor window!
Way up high the narrowest slit
It soon dawned on Ted that he'd been misled
And that Dick was a devious git

It's hard to imagine Ted's fury
Discovering this heartless deception
He'd to room with a ghost, but what vexed him most
Was the telly had hopeless reception!

That must be the final straw, thought he
No! There was another!
A small person he knew was shoved in, too
Now he'd to share with his brother! [9]

Whatever became of those children?
How long in the dark did they cower?
It's a grim, spooky tale of kids rotting in jail
The Princes in the Tower

(Two hundred years ahead
Two small remains do show
Stark evidence of a heinous offense
A horrible way to go!) [10]

You may sneer at superstitions
Consider they're all in the head
Like thirteen is rated as being ill fated
It certainly was for Ted!

Stuff about Edward V

1. We know, from many sources, that Edward was taken to The Tower in 1483 on the death of his father, Edward IV, not to be seen again. No more is certain. (Ed.)
2. See previous poem "Edward IV". (Ed.) (No, not "Ted", "Ed."!)
3. He was probably still only twelve. (i) (But that doesn't scan so well.) Moreover, if he were a teenager, almost, no further evidence is required to prove he was "green/Spotty, grotty, and rude". (Ed.)
4. Gloucester arrested Rivers claiming there was a Woodville plot against him. He later declared all the children of Edward IV and Elizabeth Woodville illegitimate, and on the 26th June 1483, dethroned Edward (V) and proclaimed himself king. (ii)
5. And "Prince of Wales" (ii)
6. Earl Rivers was Anthony Woodville, his mother's brother. (ii)
7. Richard's eldest brother was Edward V's father, Edward IV, and he had been loyal to his brother until his brother's death in 1483 when everything changed. (ii)
8. "He who cannot anachronize does not know the time." (iii)
9. Elizabeth Woodville, and her 6 remaining children, aged from 3 to 17 years, took sanctuary in Westminster Abbey but Richard, aged 11, was seized and taken to The Tower to join Edward. (i)
10. Remains were discovered in 1674 and re-buried in an urn in Westminster Abbey by Charles II, but despite much later examinations, 1933 and 1987, they have never been convincingly identified. (ii) and (iii)

More Stuff about Edward V

(i) Hilliam, David; Kings, Queens, Bones, and Bastards; Sutton Publishing Limited; London; 1999 (Paperback).
(ii) Gardiner, Juliet, Ed; The History Today Who's Who in British History; Collins and Brown; London; 2000;
(iii) Friedrich Nietzsche (more or less); http://thinkexist.com/quotation
(iv) http://www.historic-uk.com/HistoryUK/EnglandHistory/ PrincesinTower.htm;

RICHARD III
"Dangerous Dick"

(1452 – 1485)
(r.1483 –1485)

Richard of York had a cartload of kids [1]
Dick was the runt of the litter
Whereupon this stirred him on
He resolved to be stronger and fitter!

This status did not hold him back
It just made him bolder
He'd an iron will; a penchant to kill
And a humungous chip on his shoulder [2]

By gum was he highly strung!
His moods from grey to black
Hecky thump – did he have the hump
You could see it, stuck on his back [3]

No time to mess with childhood
Growing up fast was a must
At training school he learned to be cruel
And someone you couldn't trust

His favourite lesson was fighting
He always beat the other guys
Before too long he was skilful and strong
And really big – for his size

Shirking duty in those days
Was frankly a total non-starter
Boys had to be men before they were ten
By nine he was a Knight of the Garter

Childhood friends he nurtured [4]
And titles did bestow
Future subjugates were lifelong mates
Better the devil you know

Dick's big brother was "Two Time Ted" [5]
He backed him in many a campaign
Then he'd visit his home, sit on his throne
And dream of the day when he'd reign

When contenders for a crown start jostling
Tension plainly increases
Then, when the incumbent is dead things come to a head
Just like chess – with real pieces

"Whites" were looking strong
Ted Four to Ted Five is planned
But behind their backs are the devious "Blacks"
Dangerous Dick in command!

Young "Tower Ted" was in trouble
Set to be nipped in the bud [6]
He couldn't improve on Dick's hard-hearted move
His uncle was after his blood!

Ted's castles taken, his Bishops jumped
His Knights debilitated
This figure of scorn, who'd become a mere pawn
Was hunted, snared and mated

The glory of consummate power
That was the zenith for Dick
After that thrill, things went downhill
And we're talking double quick

The Pretender Henry Tudor [7]
Was really getting him down
What a gall!- He wasn't pretending at all
He was after Dickie's crown!

By the autumn of eighty five
Dick's fate was virtually sealed
They cut to the chase and came face to face
At The Battle of Bosworth Field [8]

There's Dick in the heat of the fury
One minute running amok
Then a mighty blow... and his helmet's a halo [9]
And his chain mail's a flowing white frock

For Richard's successor
No certain nominee
So The Right of Conquest chose who to invest
Henry Tudor was he! [10]

Stuff about Richard III

1.   Richard's father was Richard of York who had (according to this source at least) 13 children of whom Richard (later III) was one. (ii)
2.   A typically (of this author) unsubtle reference to the alleged (see also "Stuff 3" below) "hunchback" Richard III; scholars now believe that the emphasis put on what was probably only a slight bodily deformity was part of the negative propaganda arising from his reputation as a murderer.(iii) The discovery, in Greyfriars, Leicester England (Richard's original burial place (vii)) of bones, in late 2012, which proved, early in 2013, to be those of Richard III confirmed the symptoms of scoliosis, a lateral curvature of the spine. (v)
3.   Not again! See also "Stuff 2" above (Ed.)
4.   After his father's death at The Battle of Wakefield in 1460 the 8 year old Richard was tutored at the Estate of his Cousin the Earl of Warwick where he made several friends including Robert Percy whose own father had fought with Richard's at Wakefield and was then imprisoned and Francis Lovell, another fatherless boy tutored at Warwick, who became a lifelong friend of Richard attaining high office. (v)
5.   See preceding poem of that name about Edward IV (Ed.) Edward IV ("Two Time Ted") was succeeded briefly (8 weeks) by his 13 year old son (see also poem "Tower Ted") but he was deposed and Richard III (his "Protector") proclaimed King. (i)
6.   The belief is widely held that Richard had Edward V (and his brother, another Richard) murdered in the tower. The debate, both historical, and scientific, on that matter seems set to continue indefinitely. (iv)
7.   Henry VII, a "Pretender" at least according to Richard III, was married to Elizabeth of York (niece of Richard III) and grandson of Henry V. (vi)
8.   Richard, the last English king to die in battle, and the last of the Plantagenet line, was killed at the Battle of Bosworth, against Henry (later VII) Tudor, in 1485 (vii)
9.   The skeleton has shown (see "Stuff 2" above) that he was killed "... by one of two vicious blows to the head, including one from a sword that nearly sliced the back of his skull off..." (viii)
10. The aforementioned Henry Tudor, now Henry VII (Ed.)

More Stuff about Richard III

(i)   Gardiner, Juliet, Ed; The History Today Who's Who in British History; Collins and Brown; London; 2000;

(ii)   http://www.tudorplace.com.ar/PLANTAGENET3.htm#Richard

(iii)   http://www.npg.org.uk/collections

(iv)   Many sources

(v)   http://www.sandraworth.com/percy.htm

(vi)   Family Tree of the British Monarchy; Encyclopaedia Britannica, 15th Edition 1994

(vii) Kerrigan, M; Who Lies Where; Fourth Estate; London 1995

(viii) http://www.smithsonianmag.com/history-archaeology/The-Battle-Over-Richard-IIIsBonesAnd-His-Reputation-190400171.html,

HENRY VII
"Haughty Henry"

(1457 – 1509)
(r.1485 –1509)

When recently re-crowned "Two Times Ted" [1]
Looked for trouble to come
Henry, fourteen, tried not to be seen
But stuck out like a very sore thumb [2]

His mentor, Uncle Jasper [3]
Feared an unsavoury fate
So they chose to flee to Brittany [4]
To stay with a family mate

Henry lived there for several years
Whilst Ted, then Dick had a reign [5]
But he knew in his heart that he'd get the lead part
He was cocky and had a good brain

When his day dawned he was ready
But "which language should he be using?" [6]
To him it seemed wrong in either tongue
It must have been very confusing!

He said; "Je'll get mes hommes together
Et nous'll arrive en-masse [7]
Et on England's turf sure as eggs are oeufs
Je'll kick his scraggy … derri ère"

Henry easily raised his army
For Dick was thought unjust
And his ascension was sealed at Bosworth Field [8]
When the tyrant bit the dust

Henry was first of The Tudors
From the Lancastrian side
And for procreations and better relations
He took Elizabeth of York for his bride [9] [10]

A nice idea on paper
Though hard to perpetuate
For he could not circumvent a deep discontent
From years of inter-house hate

Insurrections were commonplace
Ultimately kept in check
The two best known who'd covert his throne
Lambert Simnel and Perkin Warbeck [11]

For pretenders, zeal is a must
Something that Lambert was rich in
But Henry stood tall and to make him look small
Set him to work in his kitchen! [12]

Perkin's plan was dead sneaky
Lordy, did he have some gall!
He said he was none other than "Tower Ted's" brother
Who hadn't been killed after all

The men who his story attracted
Were eager to fight his campaign
But though they were willing they weren't the full shilling
Thus horribly hard to train!

You may think it doesn't matter,
That soldiers don't need to be bright
But when you're stood near to a bloke with a spear
You'll hope that he knows left from right!

Several were maimed on the parade ground
Some, we're told, even died
To the sergeant's dismay they'd turn the wrong way
And puncture the bloke by their side

They were just as bad in battle
Forgetting all they'd been taught
When the first one fell the others ran like hell
Perkin, too slow, got caught

Henry gave his rival short shrift
And one of his withering looks
Then with no more ado he had him run through
He'd already got enough cooks! [13]

112

This King had a passion for money
Which his subjects had to endure
He knew how to spot it, those that had got it
And devious ways to procure! 14

People Power? – Not likely!
Summarily squashed
For whereas he did relate to affairs of state
He despised The Great Unwashed

Just fifty years old he took ill
Precise symptoms are blurred
Perhaps something nasty was stuffed in his pasty
Did Lambert have the last word!?

For the next two years, till he died 15
He tidied his kingly affairs
And spent more than enough on churches and stuff
In the hope of an invite upstairs

When you get up to heaven
(Which surely must be your goal)
Check if he's there, you'll know by his hair
It was cut round a large pudding bowl 16

Stuff about Henry VII

1. See poem "Edward IV"
2. Henry, in 1471, was the most senior Lancaster claimant to the throne. (i)
3. Henry was brought up by William Herbert at Raglan Castle but was mentored by Jasper Tudor (who later became part of his close circle and was allowed to govern), brother of his father Edmund Tudor. (i)
4. The destination was in fact France itself, but the wind took them to Brittany. (i)
5. See poems "Edward IV" and "Richard III".
6. Henry had been in Brittany from 1471 to 1484 presumably speaking French (Ed.)
7. Having fled Brittany, (fearing betrayal – see "Stuff 11") for France Henry, and "the few remaining Lancastrians" raised an army which landed at Milford Haven. (i)
8. Henry and his army defeated Richard III at Bosworth in August 1485. (i)
9. Elizabeth (a "Yorkist" as her name implies!) was daughter of Edward IV. (i)
10. As he had sworn to do (Rennes Cathedral 25th December 1483). (i)
11. Henry lived in constant fear of York (as did his son Henry VIII [see later poem "Henry VIII] after him.) (ii) One Lambert Simnel claimed to be The Earl of Warwick, nephew of King Edward IV (iii) and Perkin Warbeck (convincingly) impersonated the younger of the Princes "murdered in The Tower" (see poem "Richard III") (ii) (However, the whole period, especially the Rose Rivalry is full of convolution and betrayal and requires much more reading than can be summed up succinctly in these notes.) (Ed.)
12. Warbeck was executed in 1499, but Simnel was freed as "harmless" and became a servant. (ii)
13. Such as Simnel! (Ed.)
14. Henry indeed raised much in tax, including, ingeniously, by declaring all of those who had opposed him at "Bosworth" traitors thus enabling him to confiscate their lands. (iv)
15. Henry lies, along with his wife Elizabeth (who had died in childbirth in 1503) in a vault rather than a raised tomb as is more common in the chapel he had built in Westminster Abbey (vi)
16. Hence the hat? (Ed.) & (v)

More Stuff about Henry VII

(i)   Gardiner, Juliet, Ed; The History Today Who's Who in British History; Collins and Brown; London; 2000;

(ii)   Seward, Desmond; BBC History Magazine; Vol. 11,no.11, November 2010

(iii)   Halliday, F.E; England, A Concise History; Thames and Hudson; London; 1995

(iv)   http://www.tudorplace.com.ar/aboutHenryVII.htm

(v)   http://www.npg.org.uk/collections/search/portraitLarge/mw03078/King-HenryVII?search=ss&firstRun=true&sText=henry+VII&LinkID=mp02144&role=sit&rNo=0

(vi)   Hilliam, D: Kings, Queens, Bones and Bastards;Sutton Publishing; Thrupp, England; 2001

C. Diaz

Henry VIII
"Henry the Grrr'eighth"

(1491 – 1547)
(r.1509 – 1547) [1]

Which of our kings is most famous?
Who fascinates, shocks and beguiles?
The votes are in – it's a clear-cut win
Henry the Grrr'eighth – by miles!

What'd he got that's so special?
Umpteen wives and a massive physique
Yes, that in part, plus a marble heart
And an icy, ruthless streak

His father had died in fifteen-o-nine
Whilst quite short in the tooth
Which served to annoy his fun-loving boy
Still revelling in his youth

He'd visit the common people
He boasted kind and fair
Interested in what could better their lot
At first he seemed to care

He accepted, with grace, the laws of the land
Commending those that made them
But added one more, unwritten law
That he, being King, could break them

Aragon's Kate was already installed [2]
She'd become wife number one
And Henry popped in now and again
With some seed, so she'd grow him a son

He was fond of formidable Kate
But her potency came into doubt
Though able to pass a strong, healthy lass
No vital boy came out!

A bitter pill for Henry!
How would his bloodline survive?
When some look upon it they get a bee in their bonnet
But he'd got the whole blooming hive!

Anyway, she'd got to go
Much to her bitter chagrin
And Cranmer enforced a quickie divorce [3]
So Henry could wed Anne Boleyn [4]

They seemed a trifle late
As her bump at the wedding made clear
The expectant Anne swore to her man
"The prince you crave will appear"

The scene of the birth, soon after
Caused one of his raging fits
Ann was reviled – She'd born him a child
Without any dangly bits!

Henry counselled God
Who said the union was blighted!
So, with a swish and kerplunk Ann's head and her trunk
Were quickly disunited

Jane Seymour followed on [5]
Undaunted by his vast girth
She'd soon to agree to be number three
And set about giving birth

The royal male duly arrived
But ecstasies turned to sorrows
Childbirth's strain was too much for Jane
Who forfeited her tomorrows

Not a good time for Henry
For his enemies, even worse
Now bitterness did reign as he became
Rampageous, cruel and perverse

Henry was quick to anger
And Lordy could he vent it
In the midst of a strop if he threatened the chop
You had better believe he meant it!

The ugliness of Anne of Cleves [6]
Occasioned swift divorce
He'd soon had the lass put out to grass
So she'd only frighten his horse

Katie Howard was transferred in [7]
He felt compelled to like her
Number five had verve and drive
A young, vivacious striker!

But Henry was past his best
So his passes went astray
With reckless gall and risking her all
She scored more often playing away!

Cuckold, right under his nose
He'd become a laughing stock
So she, her lovers and hundreds of others
Took their turn on the block

That headless wayward birdie
Had left the door ajar
Now for fairer ways in twilight days
He hooked a Katherine Parr [8]

Katherine was his anchor
Supportive, sound and true
She caused no harm, exuded charm
And survived him too!

The irony of Henry's story?
His weak son soon lay dead
And conspiring fates had transferred his traits
To Bess, his daughter, instead [9]

Stuff about Henry VIII

1. The title "King of Ireland" was added to "King of England" when, in 1642, Henry VIII forced Ireland's government to declare him King of Ireland (where the Pope was still considered "Head of State").(i)

2. Catherine of Aragon (1485 – 1536) was Henry's first wife from 1509 – 1533 when the marriage was annulled by Cranmer (see "Stuff 3"). Before she married Henry she was the wife of Prince Arthur who died. The only surviving child was a daughter Mary (I [Tudor]) born in 1516. (ii)

3. Thomas Cranmer (1489 – 1556) was Archbishop of Canterbury (1533 to 1556) and argued theologically for Henry's annulment but after Henry's death was convicted of treason and heresy and despite recantations was burnt at the stake. (ii)

4. Anne Boleyn (?1501 – 1536) was Henry's second wife, married (in secret) in 1533 (probably betrothed since 1527) Their first child, later that year, was Elizabeth (I). Anne Boleyn was divorced for alleged adultery then executed in 1566. (iii)

5. Jane Seymour (?1509 – 1537) became Henry's third wife when they married in 1536, two days after Anne's execution; Jane had been in the service of both Catherine and Anne. Her son (later to become Edward VI) was born in 1537 but, to Henry's grief, she died soon afterwards. (iii)

6. Anne [Anna] of Cleves (1515 – 1557), from a strategically important area of the Low Countries, became Henry's fourth wife in January 1540. But Henry loathed her at first sight (he said she did not look at all like Holbein's portrait) and he had the marriage was annulled 6 months later. (ii) She agreed to the divorce and received a generous settlement including income, property and status but nevertheless her remaining years (ten after Henry's death) saw a decline into financial worry, a wish to return to Cleves, and death aged 42 (old for her sex, although she had not endured the, often fatal, risks of childbirth). (iv)

7. C[K]atherine Howard (1521 – 1542) was Henry's fifth wife, married in 1540 when he was 48 and she just 19. "She was racy young lady..." who failed to see the dangers of her affairs after marriage. She consoled Henry over his problem with Anne of Cleves but her adultery was revealed and she, and her lovers, were executed at the order of "...a grief stricken Henry..." in 1542. (ii)

8. Catherine Parr (1512 – 1548) was the sixth wife, married 1543. She had been widowed twice, but had a happy marriage with Henry who became her third husband to die. She re-married but died in childbirth only a year after Henry's death. (ii)

9. "Bess" was to become Elizabeth I (Ed.)

More Stuff about Henry VIII

(i) http://www.historyonthenet.com/Chronology/timelinenorthernireland.htm

(ii) Gardiner, Juliet, Ed; The History Today Who's Who in British History; Collins and Brown; London; 2000;

(iii) Gardiner, Juliet and Wenborn, N, Eds; The History Today Companion to British History; Collins and Brown; London; 1995.

(iv) Fraser, Antonia; The Six Wives of Henry VIII; Weidenfeld & Nicholson; London; 1992

EDWARD VI
"TB Ted"

(1537 – 1553)
(r. 1547 – 1553)

To live in a big man's shadow
Is always a lot to ask
For sickly Ted – who looked underfed
It proved an impossible task

His pater was notably greater [1]
In character, strength and size
Ted didn't compare, though, to be fair
The lad was pious and wise [2]

Matters of mind and soul
That's where his interest lay
To obviate fools he built grammar schools
Which bear his name to this day [3]

Nine's too young to be king
So his uncle Ed took the helm
With the grand epithet; "Duke of Somerset
Protector of the Realm" [4]

Ed was a truly good egg
Loyal to Ted and unsoiled
But a chief dissenter exposed his soft centre [5]
Dudley was bad and hard-boiled!

John Dudley, The Earl of Warwick
Think of bad traits, he'd got them
In his dark days his grasping ways
Plummeted us to rock bottom

Ted, far from well, was under Dud's spell [6]
Subject to his powerful will
Already a weed he went further to seed [7]
Fifteen and horribly ill!

The head royal doctor conjectured
What, the heck had he got?
Wild notions and quacksalver's potions
Nothing helped a fat lot

They ruled out in-growing toenail
Whooping cough and indigestion
But was it TB or not TB? [8]
That was the burning question

Indeed, he was consumed
And gently passed away
Leaving in his wake a thumping headache
For his cousin, the hapless Jane Grey

The ferryman came a calling
"Come in Ted Vee-One!"
Henry's lifelong campaign had all been in vain
His only son was gone

There is, of course, a twist
As happens in all good tales
Ted paved the way for Lady Jane Grey [9]
Sister Mary was spitting nails!

Stuff about Edward VI

1. See poem "Henry VIII" (Ed.)
2. Pious, certainly, and absorbing all the Protestant ways of his tutors, he also put great store in Archbishop Cranmer's calling him, in a sermon, "Josiah" the Old Testament boy king of Israel. (i) & (ii)
3. Many English towns have Grammar Schools bearing the name of, and founded by, King Edward VI (including, for example, Chelmsford's "KEGS"). (Ed.)
4. Edward was only 9 when he became King (he was not, apparently, allowed to wear his spurs at his coronation in case he fell over) and his uncle Edward Seymour, Duke of Somerset became Protector and indeed the power behind the throne. (i)
5. Somerset (Edward Seymour) was overthrown in 1549 and executed in 1552 leaving John Dudley (Earl of Warwick and 1st Duke of Northumberland), who had previously "appeared" to support Seymour, to exercise power and greatly influence the King, along with his supporters, to "line his own pockets" until his health, too, along with Edward's, began to deteriorate. (ii)
6. See also "Stuff 5" (Ed.)
7. Poetic licence methinks. (Ed). Edward (that is Edward VI, not (Ed.)) enjoyed, as did his father, hunting, and he also shared his temper, but he did become increasingly ill at only 15. (i) & (ii)
8. Will Shakespeare borrowed this line
It helped to make him a star
Used to convince a trouble prince
Named after a small cigar
Once again. If you believe that ..." (Ed.)
9. But not for long because following provincial uprisings and popular acclaim Mary replaced her after only a fortnight. (ii).

More Stuff about Edward VI

(i) Schama, S ; A History of Britain (3000 BC – AD 1603); BBC Worldwide Limited; London; 2000;
(ii) Gardiner, Juliet, Ed; The History Today Who's Who in British History; Collins and Brown; London; 2000;

C. Díaz

LADY JANE GREY
"Calamity Jane"

(1537 – 1554)
(r.1553) [1]

"Have I got news for you?"
Said Mrs Grey to Jane
"King Ted is keen for you to be Queen [2]
You're going to have a reign!"

"Not on your nelly;" said Jane
"That there's a sticky wicket,
I know it's an honour but I'd soon be a gonner
I'll tell him where to stick it"

"The ball's in motion," said mum
"You'll not be able to duck it
You've valid fears but they'll fall on deaf ears
Ted's already kicked the bucket" [3]

Sure enough he had changed the order [4]
Jane was next to bat
So despite her blaspheming, kicking and screaming
Upon The Throne she sat

The problem here was Mary
(That's Ted's oldest sister)
Full of bile she could not reconcile
How the heck he'd missed her

Mary rallied her troops
Jane was cast asunder [5]
"Up the creek" in just over a week [6]
The original nine day wonder

The severing of Jane's bonce [7]
Curtailed her life in clover
Mary's Catholic side had turned the tide
She'd bowled a Maiden Over!

Stuff about Lady Jane Grey

1. Acceded to the throne 10th July 1553; replaced by Mary I 19th July; at first spared by Mary but then executed in August 1553. (i) (No wonder there is not an awful lot to say) (Ed.)
2. Lady Jane Grey was the granddaughter of Mary, queen consort of France through her marriage to Louis XII, who was Henry VIII's younger sister and one of the children of Henry VII. (ii), sister of Henry VIII and great niece of Edward VI who engineered the throne to Jane and away from his sister Mary (not the Mary Tudor that was Jane's grandmother – all very confusing (Ed.)) who became Queen Mary I ("Bloody Mary") after Jane's execution. (i) (ii) and (iv). See also poems "Edward VI" and "Mary I". (Ed.)
3. Edward VI died in July 1553 (aged 15) after suffering coughing, fevers, and general wasting away. There are poison theories and "straightforward" lung disease theories. (iii)
4. See "Stuff 2".
5. Despite the support of the politicians enjoyed by Jane the "people" were against the removal of the Tudor half sister Mary I, daughter of Henry VIII and Mary replaced Jane on 19th July.(iv)
6. This phrase may have come from "Haslar [salt] Creek" in Portsmouth harbour ("salt" may be the origin of another name for the creek). Wounded sailors during Nelson's time, were taken there to be admitted to the Royal Naval Hospital Haslar. Despite being held prisoner to prevent desertion some tried to escape through the sewers to the creek. Without a paddle this would be hopeless, as in "up the creck without a paddle". (Author)
7. See "Stuff 1".

More Stuff about Lady Jane Grey

(i)   Gardiner, Juliet, Ed; The History Today Who's Who in British History; Collins and Brown; London; 2000;

(ii)   Encyclopædia Britannica; 15th Edition 1994; Family Tree of The British Monarchy; 1994 and http://chaos1.hypermart.net/fullsize/ftbritmonfs.gif

(iii) http://en.wikipedia.org/wiki/Edward_VI_of_England#Illness_and_death;

(iv) http://en.wikipedia.org/wiki/Mary_Tudor,_Queen_of_France;

C. Díaz

MARY I [1]
Bloody Mary

(1516-1558)
(r.1553 –1558

Mary, Mary, quite contrary
How did your Queenship go?
History tells of chock-a-block cells
Executions all in a row

The crime? – The wrong religion! [2]
Three hundred put to the flame [3]
By this brutal campaign she attracted disdain
And her "Bloody" nickname

She even had her niece executed [4]
Which wasn't very fair
Jane, as it goes, had got right up her nose
By sitting in her chair [5]

Mary married King Phillip of Spain [6]
To further her Catholic cause
A bitter insult which had to result
In Protestants sharpening their claws

Those who stood against her
Weren't easy to suppress
As they put their weight behind their candidate
Her younger sister, Bess [7]

The Queen got wind of the rebellion [8]
And being as she had the power
Acted with haste to have Bess disgraced
And locked her up in The Tower [9]

The one in London, not Blackpool
It was dark and Bess was afraid
There was no romancing or ballroom dancing
Nor an amusement arcade!

131

Mary seemed to relent and implored her
"Come to Hatfield House 'as my guest'"
From where Bess stood that sounded quite good
But it really meant "house arrest"

Why? you must be asking
"Was Mary acting so mild?"
She'd lost her figure, her tummy was bigger
She thought she was with child [10]

With her very own heir in the making
Bess couldn't be any harm
But Mary's good cheer would soon disappear
Her lump was a false alarm [11]

Historians think an ovarian cyst [12]
Befell our poorly royal
To her doctor's dismay she faded away
And quit this mortal coil

Stuff about Mary I

1. Apart from the soubriquet "Bloody Mary" Mary I is often referred to as "Mary Tudor", being a daughter of the Tudor King, Henry VIII (and Catherine of Aragon). (Ed.)
2. Mary had always refused to abandon the Catholic liturgy, particularly during the reign of her half-brother Edward VI. (i)
3. During the second year of her reign her opposition to non-Catholics grew in intensity with her power and a year after that, after the restoration of the heresy laws in 1555, she "became committed to persecution which included 300 burnings". (i)
4. Mary imprisoned Lady Jane Grey in 1554 after the suppression of the rebellion. (i) (see also "Stuff 8").
5. She (Jane Grey) had indeed sat in Mary's "chair", but that "chair" just happened to be The Throne of England! (Ed.)
6. Phillip, the Catholic King of Spain, came to London to marry Mary in 1554 in a marriage intended to forge an alliance between Britain and Spain. (i)
7. Bess (later Elizabeth I) was always in a dangerous position vis à vis Mary and she was imprisoned in 1554 although "... nothing was ever proved to link her with Protestant conspiracies ..." (i)
8. That is the rebellion led by Sir Thomas Wyatt in 1554. (i)
9. See "Stuff 7"
10. As was always the way at the time a male heir was hoped for and, in her case, one to continue the Catholic line. (Ed.)
11. She was not, after all, with child. (i)
12. In 1557, and England joined Spain in war with France, only to lose Calais at the beginning of 1558; Mary died later that year after another false pregnancy which may have been a cyst or stomach cancer. (i)

More Stuff about Mary I

(i) Gardiner, Juliet and Wenborn, N, Eds; The History Today Who's Who in British History; Collins and Brown; London; 1995.

ELIZABETH I
Bess – The Virgin Queen

(1533 – 1603)
(r. 1558 – 1603)

Beneath a womanly shell
A core as hard as rock
Strong and keen this dynamic queen
Was a chip off a granite block

She wasn't a happy child
I hear you ask "how come?"
Well, listen mate, it's not so great
If dad decapitates mum [1]

Bess was banished from court
But luckily didn't go far
Because when Henry was cold she came back to the fold
Cared for by Catherine Parr [2]

The Crown was a distant dream
Two others kept her at bay
But the deaths of "TB" and Bloody Mary [3] [4]
Rapidly cleared the way

Before she'd even settled in
And been officially crowned
Foreign speakers and power seekers
Arrived to sniff around

Suitors came from far and wide
To win her love and trust
She didn't much go for marriage though
And wasn't all that fussed

She exuded vestal virtue
"For God and the Nation"
Though from what we glean "The Virgin Queen"
Was a gross exaggeration!

There were some special men, you see
The first was Robert Dudley [5]
He was very polite, charming and bright
Handsome, suave and cuddly

The Earl of Essex betrayed her [6]
Which it seems she didn't like
So, instead of his head beside her in bed
She had it stuck on a spike

And, of course, the suave explorer
With whom she'd spoon and dally
Without whose trips, we'd not have chips
Swashbuckling Walter Raleigh [7]

Philip of Spain, with alliance in mind [8]
Made a romantic bid
He gave her jewels and gardening tools
And a ticket to watch Real Madrid

Our Queen wasn't so easily bought
She wouldn't share her crown
Added to which, another small hitch
She supported Luton Town!

Marriage seemed a hopeless dream
All chances turned and fled
By the time she'd decide to be Dudley's bride
He'd wed someone else instead [9]

So, she betrothed herself to her subjects
And to prove it was no idle boast
With severe garb and a look macabre
Had the appearance of a ghost

With strength of vision and firm belief
Her ministers had this brief;
"Avoid fruitless wars, make employment laws
And measures for Poor Relief"

With her Foreign Policy
Thirty years of peace, we'd had
But then Phillip heard an event had occurred
That made him hopping mad

The matter here in question
That got Phil tied in knots
Was the horrid fate of his Catholic mate
Mary Queen of Scots [10]

She'd been expelled from Scotland
In fifteen sixty eight
And bum of bummers it took nineteen summers
To decide on Mary's fate

The decision finally struck Bess
Whilst in the garden strolling
And at Fotheringay, the very next day
Another head went rolling

"The woman's gone too far", said Phil
"I'm a man and much, much harder
I'll make some notes, then I'll send my boats
And I'll call them – "an Armada!"

He'd not reckoned on our Bess though
Marching on the beaches
Our feisty Queen; tough yet serene
Was making rousing speeches

She said; "I have the heart and stomach of a King [11]
I don't like the French or the Spanish either
I'm the boss and if they make me cross
I'll sell my villa in Ibiza"

Her guts and spirit won the day
The Spanish were found lacking
They were seasick as well and when night fell
She'd sent the Armada packing [12]

She ruled on with purpose and strength
England's mentor and her sage
And such was the progress made by Bess
We call it "The Golden Age"

When she finally passed away
The people mourned their Queen
For in her day it's fair to say
"Elizabeth reigned supreme"

Stuff about Elizabeth I

1. Elizabeth's mother was Anne Boleyn, second wife of Henry VIII and executed on his orders in 1536. (ii)
2. Catherine Parr (1512 – 1548) was Henry VIII's sixth and last wife, she looked after numerous step children including the future Queen Elizabeth I. (i)
3. "TB" is a reference to Edward VI who was Henry VIII's son by Jane Seymour, who died of tuberculosis ("TB"), or possibly pneumonia, in 1547 aged 16, in 1553, after a reign of only 6 years. (i)
4. "Bloody Mary" (Mary I) reigned. 1553 – 1558 (b.1516 – d. 1558) was the daughter of Henry VIII and Catherine of Aragon (see elsewhere), she was not allowed to see her mother from 1531 and was bastardized on the annulment of the marriage. An Act of Parliament (1544) saw her restored to second in line after her half-brother Edward VI. She was strongly Catholic and the heresy laws, restored in 1555, led to 300 burnings. Against the Pope's wishes she married her cousin, Phillip II (see above) in 1554. She died, possibly of stomach cancer, in 1558. (i)
5. Robert Dudley (1532/3 – 1588) was an enemy of Mary I and had been brought up in the Courts of Henry VIII and Edward VI and had known Elizabeth I for a long time. His status as a favourite declined when he accepted honours from the Dutch in 1885 but Elizabeth mourned his death, from a malarial infection, in 1588. (i)
6. The Earl of Essex (1566 – 1601) referred to was Robert Devereaux the 19th Earl. Always controversial, granting knighthoods against the Queen's wishes, disobeying military superiors he fell from all favour after a particularly costly Irish campaign in 1600. His coup, against Elizabeth in 1601 failed, and he was executed. (i)
7. Sir Walter Raleigh (1554 – 1618) was a man of short temper, often in trouble for affray. He rose high in Court and in Elizabeth's esteem but fell into disgrace when the Earl of Essex (see above), his main of many enemies, revealed Raleigh's secret marriage to the wrong Liz, Elizabeth Throckmorton, a maid of honour. Elizabeth's jealous rage saw Raleigh in the Tower but he outlived her, finally meeting his execution after continuing to annoy too many powerful people. (i)
8. Phillip II of Spain, r.1556 –1598 (b.1527 –d.1598). As the husband of Mary I he was King (Consort) of England from 1554 but lost all rights on Mary's death. He "tepidly" offered marriage to Elizabeth but his third and fourth wives (Mary had been his second) were French and Austrian. Relations with England deteriorated into long term, but undeclared war. (i)
9. Robert Dudley (see above) had numerous affairs despite his need to keep the favour of Elizabeth; he was desperate for an heir and may have married "someone else instead". (ii) Lady Douglas (or

alternatively, Douglass) (iii) Sheffield (?1545 1605) bore him two sons but it is not certain whether she married Dudley. (i)

10. Mary Queen of Scots (b.1542 d.1587) was Queen of Scotland 1542 – 1567 (crowned at the age of 6 days on the death of her father James V (of Scotland) and Queen of France (1559 – 1560) but lost her French crown on the death of her husband Francis II. A Catholic struggling in an increasingly Protestant Scotland she was defeated in battle and deposed in 1567, imprisoned, escaped, defeated again, and fled to England where she was implicated in the murder of her husband, and father of the future James VI, Darnley. After 19 years, during which time Mary was imprisoned, Elizabeth I eventually overcame her reluctance to execute an anointed sovereign. (i)

11. In her speech (by William Shakespeare) at Tilbury in 1588 as England prepared for an invasion by King Philip of Spain and his powerful Armada. Elizabeth I hit head-on the allegation that a female monarch was less suited to lead a nation in wartime than a male. As a result, the speech is best known for its line "I have the body but of a weak and feeble woman; but I have the heart and stomach of a king." (iii)

12. The Armada referred to is the one of 1588 (there were several in an ongoing war with Spain). Spain faced logistical problems fighting at what, for those times, was a great distance. However, victory for the English was in no way certain, but the expected invasion was averted when an unexpected and powerful wind blew the Armada away from the English shores. (i) & (ii)

More Stuff about Elizabeth I

(i)   Gardiner, Juliet, Ed; The History Today Who's Who in British History; Collins and Brown; London; 2000.

(ii) Gardiner, Juliet and Wenborn, N, Eds; The History Today Companion to British History; Collins and Brown; London; 1995.

(iii) http://www.nationalcenter.org/ElizabethITilbury.html

C. Díaz

JAMES I (of England) and VI (of Scotland)[1]
Jim (One and Six)

(1566 – 1625)
(r. [Scotland] 1567 – 1625)
(r. [England] 1603-1625)

The son of Mary Queen of Scots [2]
For power had a thirst
In Scotland he was James the Sixth [3]
In England, James the First

Experienced? You bet he was
A veritable sage
He was ruling Scots and quelling plots
At thirteen months of age [4]

Jim was bright, and understood [5]
The lessons that he sat in
He took French and Greek and learned to speak
A smattering of Latin

With full control at seventeen
He took Draconian actions
Put uprisings down and purged the crown
Of greedy Scottish factions

His marriage to Ann of Denmark [6]
Was always doomed to fail
On paper it was fine – Kids numbered nine
But his closest friends were male! [7]

He thought his claim to The English Crown
Was fully justified [8]
He was close to Bess and had great success
Bringing her on side

Their differences were laid to rest
Shelved and left unsaid
He was only slightly peeved that Bess relieved [9]
His mother of her head

So, when Bess popped her clogs
In sixteen hundred and three
He fulfilled his aim to win his claim
And such was the decree

With the Kingdom now United
For flagpoles to adorn
A National sign from Jim's design
The Union Jack was born [10]

But Bess's death had left a void
Change is always scary
And a Scottish squirt dressed in a skirt!
Small wonder folk were wary

He regularly looked a mess
And had a shambling gait
He'd often wobble, dribble and hobble [11]
A right pathetic state!

Scotland was a breeze to rule
Here in stark contrast
Try as he may little went his way [12]
Disorders many and vast

Most notably The Gunpowder Plot
When Guy Fawkes dropped a clanger
That's the night he failed to light
The first and biggest banger [13]

In later years Jim courted Spain
His judgement now had faltered
His councillors raised cries against close ties
But his mind would not be altered

Then Walter Raleigh plundered Spain
Incurring Jim's wrath [14]
To upset this king was a foolhardy thing
Walt took an early bath!

Yes, Jim finished off our hero [15]
Who'd battled with the tides
That splendid bloke who bought us smoke
To clog up our insides

Jim was surely on the slide
Gaga signs on show
His hole had been dug so God pulled his plug
Come on young Charles, your go!

Though James was a learned man
And talented at school
Please don't forget his epithet
This was the "Wisest Fool" [16]

Stuff about James I & VI

1. Chronologically speaking he was James VI & I, but "Six and a penny" (6/1d) is less catchy than "One and Six" (1/6d). (Ed.)
2. Not to be confused with Mary I (Bloody Mary of England, a.k.a. Mary Tudor). (Ed.)
3. He became King of Scotland in 1567, aged 13 months, on Mary's forced abdication after a rebellion, murders, and much mayhem and shame. Passim inc. (i) & (iii)
4. Not entirely true! There was a Regent appointed by Mary, The Earl of Moray, (assassinated in 1571 (iv)) and James had various governors, tutors, and advisors throughout his minority. (i), (ii), & (iii)
5. His skills were largely used in "devious diplomacy". (i)
6. In 1581 he, with the help of "the first of many attractive male favourites", overthrew the then Regent, the Earl of Merton. (i)
7. He went to Denmark to collect his bride in 1590 displaying "an uncharacteristic heterosexual ardour". (i)
8. Largely because his great grandmother was Henry VII's daughter who had married James IV of Scotland. (i)
9. James had never known Mary, Queen of Scots, she having been executed when he was only a year old. (Ed.)
10. The flag was designed by James and became official, by Royal Decree, in 1606. (v)
11. He may have had mild cerebral palsy (i) (Not, in those days, afforded the sympathy due to it. (Ed).
12. "A coarse conceited pedant without any understanding of the English people" (vi) James upset Parliament which raised an "accumulation of grievances", there were problems with the Royal Budget, and he annoyed the existing titled classes with a plethora of new honours. (i)
13. Guy (Guido) Fawkes had been betrayed by other Catholics unwilling to see their friends (in Parliament) killed had he succeeded. (i)
14. James had opposed war with Spain but his ban on profiteering buccaneering expeditions did not stop Raleigh from plundering Spanish ships, not to mention his conspiring to overthrow James. The result was his imprisonment in the Tower in 1604. (i)
15. James relented in 1616 allowing Raleigh to lead a Guiana expedition but that ended in mutiny and failure, and Raleigh was, on his return to England, executed. (i)
16. Sir Anthony Weldon, 17th Century courtier and politician, is said to have applied this epithet to James meaning him wise in small things but a fool in greater things. (vii)

More Stuff about James I & VI

(i)   Gardiner, Juliet, Ed; The History Today Who's Who in British History; Collins and Brown; London; 2000;

(ii)   Various Eds; The Concise Dictionary of National Biography; Oxford University Press; Oxford; 1994;

(iii) Schama, S; A History of Britain (3000 BC – AD 1603); BBC Worldwide Limited; London; 2000;

(iv) http://en.wikipedia.org/wiki/James_Stewart,_1st_Earl_of_ Moray;

(v)   http://en.wikipedia.org/wiki/Union_Flag;

(vi) Halliday, F. E; England: A Concise History; Thames and Hudson Limited; London; 1989;

(vii) http://en.wikipedia.org/wiki/Anthony_Weldon;

CHARLES I
"Chopped Charles"

(1600 – 1649)
(r. 1625 – 1649)

When James the first had passed away
Son Charles was next in the queue
And with all good grace, he took his place
To see what he could do

"I want my Charles to be 'The First'"
Said Anne, his meddling mother [1]
So they checked the book, and she was in luck
Because there hadn't been another

Young Charles was weak and sickly [2]
Sustained by his God
Lonely, forlorn and extremely withdrawn
He was a miserable little … boy

Sensitive though, and virtuous [3]
With a charming manner
But courage he'd lack and often hold back
Af-f-flicted by his s-stammer [4]

Five foot four, lank hair, gaunt face
These images evoke
A pointy beard to chin adhered
A scrawny little bloke!

He demanded wealth and power
And the baubles that it brings
It was ill conceived, but he strongly believed
In The Divine Right of Kings [5]

He would not have his judgement questioned [6]
He thought Parliament a joke
His many faults encouraged revolts
He scorned the common folk

Henrietta Maria, his only wife
Was trouble from the start [7]
But this French Royal was dutifully loyal
Right till he came apart [8]

Three sons, and healthy too
She managed to attain
The usual names, Charles, Henry and James,
Two went on to reign

Charles needed his subjects' money
His wars and excesses to feed
With that in mind he robbed them blind
A groat on a pint of mead!

Folk had to pay his Ship Tax [9]
Jail for those in arrears!
And when Parliament moaned he packed them off home [10]
For the next eleven years

When they returned to the Commons
The gulf between them was vaster
He, condescending and sour – They, demanding more power
A recipe for disaster!

So, the conflict twixt Parliament and Crown
As his father had fashioned before
Split the population and led a divided Nation
Into bloody Civil War

Charles commanded The Cavaliers
But didn't go to the front
He'd soon have been dead if attacked by a Roundhead [11]
He was only a little runt!

Cromwell, who led the Roundheads
Didn't lead from HQ [12]
He most liked it when he could tackle the enemy
And run his sword through a few

Cavaliers got off to a corker
Fighting with valour and skill
Said Ollie; "That wasn't fair, we'd no time to prepare
And they had the top of Edge Hill"

So he formed his New Model Army [13]
And his military problems were cured
By Marston Moor in sixteen forty four
It was the Royalists' turn to get skewered

At Naseby just one year later
They'd fired the final shots
A bloody defeat, ignoble retreat
And Charles took refuge with the Scots

That was a huge mistake!
Fact is, he was worth a few quid
He couldn't imagine they'd turn him in
But, as it turned out – they did!

His life was in Cromwell's hands
Not a safe place to be!
With scant good reason, the charge was treason
"Guilty" the judge's decree

To question the verdict was useless
So he didn't bother to ask it
The axe was keen – Charles was calm and serene
Right 'til his head hit the basket

This was a terrible day for Royalists
Many were driven to tears
Cromwell had his way and kept Monarchs at bay
But for just eleven years [14]

Cromwell, the big old softie
Knew Charles' kin were fraught
So with cotton and thread sewed back his head
What a lovely thought! [15]

Stuff about Charles I

1. For this assertion there is, the author admits, no evidence other than the reasoning that 'All mothers meddle, therefore Charles' mother must have meddled'. (Ed.)
2. During his early years Charles suffered from very poor health, lack of parental affection, and a pronounced stammer (i)
3. Possibly attributable to his surrounding himself by chaplains and admiring their "sacramentalist and ceremonialist piety".(ii)
4. See "Stuff 2"
5. The Divine Right of Kings (meaning the king is subject to no-one on earth, only to God: (Ed) was classically set out in a book by Charles' father, James I, in a book intended for Charles' brother (who was next in line, but died before acceding), called "The True Law of Free Monarchies" (1598). (iii)
6. As might be expected from a man who believed he was second only to God. (See stuff 5.) (Ed.)
7. A marriage for diplomatic reasons (allowing England a share of French, if not Spanish, power)(iii) meant, just as would have a Spanish marriage, a Catholic Queen, and it seemed to the Protestant population that Charles listened only to himself and to her. (iv)
8. Henrietta Maria had actually returned to France in 1644 after the wars had turned very much against Charles (e.g. Marston Moor) but after his coming apart (the author's subtle way of describing the separation of his head from his body) in 1649 she was left destitute. (i)
9. A tax that Charles levied without the consent of Parliament, which instead of being only applied to coastal towns in wartime, was collected inland, to an extent provoking The Civil Wars. (v)
10. He had already dismissed Parliament in 1629 and it did not meet again throughout his "Eleven Years' Tyranny" (ii)
11. The followers of Cromwell were known as "Roundheads" because of the short hair favoured by some of the Puritans amongst them, whereas "Cavaliers" (originally from "Chevalier" or "horseman" (vi)) but coming to be an insult implying a "dandified" attitude . (Ed.)
12. Many sources describe Cromwell as being a leader "from the front". (Ed.)
13. Many politicians, in 1644, held high army ranks and some had been blamed for previous losses. At Cromwell's behest, and after months of negotiation, the politicians/soldiers resigned their commissions and a fresh start was made with the "New Model Army". (vii)
14. Cromwell died in 1658, his son Richard lacked his father's charisma, the Republic collapsed and the monarchy was restored. (ii)
15. After the execution Cromwell ordered Charles's head to be sewn back on "so his family could pay their respects.(viii)

More Stuff about Charles I

(i)   http://www.bbc.co.uk/history/British/civil_war_revolution/personality _charles_01.shtml;

(ii) Gardiner, Juliet, Ed; The History Today Who's Who in British History; Collins and Brown; London; 2000;

(iii) Kishlansky, Mark; A Monarchy Transformed; Penguin; London; 1997.

(iv) Schama, S; A History of Britain (The British Wars); BBC; London, 2001.

(v)   http://en.wikipedia.org/wiki/Ship_money;

(vi) http://en.wikipedia.org/wiki/Cavalier;

(vii) Ashley, M; The English Civil Wars; Sutton Publishing, Gloucestershire, England; 1992.

(viii) Many sources state this as fact and it would be wrong to cite any one of them as definitive.

OLIVER CROMWELL
LORD PROTECTOR of ENGLAND

"Ollie"

(1599 – 1658)
(Protector 1649 – 1658)

A young life of peace and comfort
For which he'd parents to thank
They owned some land, were reasonably grand
And had a few quid in the bank

Ollie stood out from nine siblings [1]
A grafter and far from dumb
But how could they have known that when fully grown
What a very big "Whig" he'd become [2]

His father died pretty young
And uncle soon followed suit [3]
The young man had no qualms as he managed two farms
And proved to be very astute

He loathed it when people suffered
Oppressed by tax-hungry Kings
Though friends thought him barmy he enlisted in the army [4]
Resolved to change some things

Ollie had all you could ask for
Traits and qualities most needed then
A shrewd politician; a military tactician
A natural "Chief of Men" [5]

Determined and ambitious
Driven by power divine
To God he gave thanks as he rose through the ranks
Command his grand design [6]

His battlefield skills were admired
Incisive, astute and cunning
He reached his peak and won "Commander of the Week" [7]
For a stunning twelve weeks running

He formed his New Model Army [8]
To bring errant Charles to heel
Those that he chose were war hardened pros
Charged with religious zeal

Far too good for The Cavaliers [9]
The army of the Royals
Charles and his son were forced to run
The victor takes the spoils!

Ollie's farms proved a welcome relief
When hostilities came to an end
Fields to harrow, muck to barrow
And several fences to mend

Charles was branded a traitor
His attitude hadn't improved
His haughty poses got up peoples noses
So his head was duly removed

Now England needed a helmsman
A leader for when they got stuck
A firm stand taker; a decision-maker
Someone who'd stop the buck

Cromwell was the obvious choice
His interview style impressed
Plus, his voice was so loud he stood out in a crowd
Not a man to get stressed!

With God as his strength and reason
He answered The Nation's call
Direct and intense and with no pretence
They'd got him "Warts and all" [10]

It was hard to choose a handle
Some favoured calling him "King"
After a few jars of mead it was finally agreed
"Lord Protector" had a nice ring [11]

Said Ollie; "We all have our different opinions
I want each man to have his say
Get your thoughts off your chest; you decide what's best
Then we'll do it my way!"

Though his style didn't suit everybody
He steadfastly followed this theme
By some he was hated, but his resolve created
A stable civilian regime

When assessing this man's contribution
Should you despise or adore him?
Sullied or pure, one thing's for sure,
You certainly can't ignore him!

Ollie was "late" in sixteen fifty eight
The Commonwealth was floored [12]
When it lacked the vigour of this towering figure
The Monarchy was restored [13]

***

He was laid to rest intact
'Cos he'd 'sort of' been elected
But then three years later, branded a traitor
His head was disconnected! [14]

Stuff about Oliver Cromwell

1. Of the ten children born to the Cromwells, seven survived (a high number for the times): Oliver was the only boy. (ii)
2. "The Whigs" was Cromwell's political party. [Ed.]
3. The uncle here was his mother's brother, "another well to do farmer". (ii)
4. He was involved in the formation of the Eastern Counties Association authorised by Parliament for the raising of troops and supplies. (ii)
5. From the title of Antonia Fraser's book (ii)
6. He was known to spend the night, before battle, in prayer. (ii)
7. Well known for his skilled military strategies including the use of cavalry and cannon. (ii)
8. The "New Model Army" (Cromwell only played a part in its formation) comprised 33,000 paid men, formed in 1644/5 and often mocked by the Royalists because of the mixed character of the infantry.(iii)
9. "Cavaliers" the name applied to the King's men is not as chivalrous as it sounds, is from the Spanish, caballeros, mocking their alleged allegiance to Spain and Roman Catholicism. The Parliamentarians were known as Roundheads after the short hair style in favour at the beginning of the Wars.(ii)
10. After the abolition of the monarchy in 1649 the Puritans (Cromwell at their head) expected everyone, artists included, to adopt a plain, unadorned style. Cromwell instructed one of his many portraitists, Dutch artist Peter Lely to include all his [Cromwell's], pimples, warts, and everything as he saw him.(iii)
11. This also gave him supreme Legal and Executive powers. (i)
12. With the abolition of the monarchy England became a "Commonwealth". (Ed.)
13. His son Richard (The Protectorship was hereditary) took over for less than a year but lacked his father's charisma and determination to maintain the Protectorate. (i)
14. In 1660 Charles II, the first of the restored monarchs, had Cromwell's body exhumed and ceremonially executed; his head is buried in Sydney Sussex College Chapel, Cambridge, England. (ii)

More Stuff about Oliver Cromwell

(i)   Gardiner, Juliet, Ed; The History Today Who's Who in British History; Collins and Brown; London; 3000.

(ii) Fraser, Antonia; Cromwell Our Chief of Men; Random House UK Limited; London; 1993

(iii) Ashley, Maurice; The English Civil War; Sutton Publishing Limited; Bridgend, G.B.; 1998

C. Díaz

CHARLES II
"Cheeky Charlie"

(1630 – 1685)
(r.1660 – 1685)

This was "The Merrie Monarch" [1]
Read on to learn the truth
Of a King of leisure and pleasure
A lecherous cad, forsooth!

His elder brother, who'd died [2]
Left him first in the kingly queue
But after The Civil War had raged, the throne was engaged!
He was bursting, but what could he do?

As you'll know from previous reading
Cromwell had taken his pew
Who when asked to vacate said; "Listen mate,
The only throne you'll get's the loo"

Said Charles, in reply to this rudeness
"You're a man with no breeding or grace,
Your behaviour's appalling and though I don't like name-calling,
You're a proper "Warty Face" [3]

He raised an army in Scotland [4]
Resolved to return and reign
But he didn't get far and at Worcester and Dunbar
Was beaten again – and again [5]

Pounded to submission
Charles was forced to flee
In a mighty close scrape and to aid his escape
He reputedly hid in a tree! [6]

Taking refuge over in France
He moped in abject misery
He'd a job treading grapes, learned to toss crêpes
And was Pluto at Euro Disney [7]

He then made a treaty with Spain [8]
Which helped to ease his sorrow
And, being lazy as hell, it suited him well
How they put things off 'til tomorrow

When Cromwell's son Richard replaced him
The writing was on the wall
It was clear at a glance that he hadn't a chance
The twerp was no use at all! [9]

England had come off the rails
It needed to get back on track
Though horribly divided they finally decided
To give kings another crack

Charles made the most of his new post
Combining work and leisure
An occasional meeting, gourmet eating
But mostly carnal pleasure!

To say that he liked the ladies
Would be vastly understated
London's foremost dandy was immoral and randy
Decadence seldom abated

A barren wife in Catherine [10]
But mistresses aplenty!
The exact amount? – Statisticians lost count
Officially almost twenty [11]

"That Nell Gwynn's my favourite" [12]
To his mates he'd swank and boast "
She's an orange seller but, as a red-blooded feller
It's her melons that interest me most!"

Fourteen recorded offspring
Whose family lines live on
Here's something though that you may not know
Princess Di was descended from one!

The Black Death struck in sixty five [13]
The blame fell to The Crown
Then, curse upon curse, matters got worse
When most of London burnt down [14]

Edward Hyde, the King's advisor [15]
Was the fall guy to quell a revolt
When Charles had done he'd convinced everyone
That both things were Edward's fault

Titus Oates planned Charlie's demise
The Popish Plot the crime [16]
You know from these notes Charles had quite enough oats
To last a whole lifetime

Charles's dotage was tranquil
Stresses and strains had eased
He'd plenty of cash, no need to be rash
In fact, he did just as he pleased

Apart from improvements in The Navy [17]
His feats were precious few
But, with no-one better to come, the people kept schtum
Better the Devil they knew!

This wayward King was ailing
A problem lurked inside
An apoplectic fit at fifty four and a bit
And with one final stroke ... he died [18]

To mark Charles's Restoration
(And Parliamentarian folly)
The twenty ninth of May is "Oak Apple Day"
The tree where he hid from Ollie

Stuff about Charles II

1. Charles was popularly known as the "Merrie Monarch", in reference to both the liveliness and hedonism of his court, and his repeal of Cromwell's laws forbidding much pleasure. (i)
2. Charles II would have had an elder brother but he, Charles James, Duke of Cornwall and Rothsay, was stillborn in May 1629. (ix)
3. Cromwell certainly had warts; see poem "Oliver Cromwell" "Stuff 10". (Ed.)
4. After the execution of his father, Charles I, in 1649, Charles (II) was proclaimed King of Britain in Edinburgh (also in Ireland in Royalist towns) and it was, therefore, not surprising that he chose Scotland in which to raise and army to invade England and take the Crown. (ii)

5. Some of Charles' losses are attributable in part to the lack of support he received in the north of England where there was a "deep-dyed" dislike of the Scots. (iii)

6. The "Royal Oak" (many English pubs are now so named Ed.) was at Boscobel in Shropshire, not far from his scene of defeat at Worcester. (v)

7. No comment! (Ed.)

8. At the Treaty of Brussels, signed by Charles II on The 2nd April 1656 (Cromwell having obtained the French agreement to stop their support for him) the Spanish agreed to provide an army of invasion as soon as the Royalists could secure an English port for their disembarkation. (x)

9. Oliver Cromwell's son, Richard (1626 – 1712) was Lord Protector of England from September 1658 to May 1659 but abdicated and fled the country on the Restoration (of Charles II) but had never been anything like his father and he was not up to the job which he had inherited. (vi)

10. Charles married Catherine of Breganza in 1651. She was a Portuguese princess which annoyed the Spanish and thus pleased the French. No children were produced. (vi)

11. Numbers vary between sources but there were certainly many. Ed. Known as "Old Rowley", after a contemporary Whitehall goat, known for its "lasciviousness", Charles himself once, allegedly, claimed 39, which being "…the number of Articles of the Anglican Faith" was right for the "Head of the Church of England". (vi)

12. Nell Gwynn, "a young, lively comic actress at The Drury Lane Theatre, was one of the best known and popular, amongst the people, would have been ennobled along with many other mistresses had Charles not died shortly before she did. (vi)

13. The "Black Death", [or perhaps, more correctly "The Great Plague of London" (ii)] was another rat flea borne epidemic (although cats and dogs were blamed at the time (vii)) and was seen, particularly when coupled with the wars that preceded it and the Great Fire of London which followed, as God's punishment of a sinful country (including by Anglicans for the acceptance of Catholicism). (ii)

14. "During the night of 2nd September 1666 the Great Fire broke out. It was to rage for four days and nights causing more damage [though few lives were lost] than any similar calamity until the great blitz of 1940 – 42." (iv)

15. Edward Hyde (1609 – 1674) became Earl of Clarendon when accompanying his ally, Charles II back to London. For various reasons he made enemies in Parliament and Court and after an unsuccessful attempt to impeach him he went into exile in France from 1667 until his death where he completed his important work A History of the Great Rebellion. (v)

16. The Popish Plot was hatched by, amongst others, Titus Oates, an anti-Catholic activist, in 1679/80 to suggest Catholics were plotting to overthrow the King. Although Oates was imprisoned he was freed at the time of The Glorious Revolution (1688/9) when Charles' successor, his brother James, was replaced by William and Mary. (v)
17. The British Navy became the Royal Navy under Charles II in 1660, when James (later James II) Charles' brother was a Lord High Admiral. Then, in 1664 the Royal Marines were formed. Charles II also founded the Royal Society of London to encourage scientific knowledge of astronomy, biology, geographical exploration, navigation and seamanship. (viii)
18. Charles died, a few days after an orgy, suffering from uraemia. On his death bed he was secretly admitted to the Roman Catholic Church and also sent apologies to his still loving wife for his bad behaviour throughout his lifetime. (vi)

More Stuff about Charles II

(i) http://en.wikipedia.org/wiki/Charles_II_of_England;
(ii) Kishlansky, M; A Monarchy Transformed (Britain 1603 – 1714);Penguin; Harmondsworth, England; 1997
(iii) Fraser, Antonia; Cromwell Our Chief of Men; Random House UK Limited; London; 1993
(iv) Latham, R. Ed; The Illustrated Pepys; Book Club Associates; London; 1978;
(v) Gardiner, Juliet and Wenborn, N, Eds; The History Today Companion to British History; Collins and Brown; London; 1995.
(vi) Hilliam, David; Kings, Queens, Bones and Bastards; Sutton Publishing Limited; Stroud, Gloucestershire, England; 1998;
(vii) Schama, S ;A History of Britain (1603 – 1776); BBC Worldwide Limited; London; 2000;
(viii) http://www.royalnavalmuseum.org/info_sheets_naval_hist ory. htm;
(ix) http://en.wikipedia.org/wiki/Charles_I_of_England;
(x) http://www.british-civil-wars.co.uk/military/anglo-spanish-war-flanders.htm ;

JAMES II (of England) an VII (of Scotland)
Jim (Two and Seven) [1]

(1633 – 1701)
(r.1685-1688)

Reports of Jim were scary [2]
Autocratic and weird
The people were frightened, anxiety heightened
Was this the Devil they feared?

Jim was raised in France
Out of Ollie's range
Dolled up in culottes, dancing endless gavottes
A recipe for "strange"

He too had a huge libido
(You'll know what that means!)
This is no work of fiction – an inbred addiction [3]
Was lurking in his genes

An army life for Jim
And steely reputation
Many a campaign against France and Spain [4]
Fighting quelled frustration!

When his brother Charles was reigning
Jim, Duke of York, had a treat
Being so blooming brave he commanded The Navy [5]
At the head of a powerful fleet

Many a battle he courageously won
Sending foes to watery graves
Conquering lands overseas with consummate ease
As England Ruled the Waves

New Amsterdam came under his fire
Soon he overthrew it [6]
Upon staking that claim it took his name
"New York" is how we know it

Jim was a Catholic right to the core
His wife was even keener
Wholly devout and a right old trout
Was Mary of Modena [7]

Charged with his strong beliefs
His subjects had to share them
And, to settle old scores, he passed pro-Catholic laws
– But Protestants wouldn't wear them [8]

So they rose up on all sides [9]
To hasten Jim's downfall
They were repressed and inclined to have axes to grind
Revolting, one and all!

Jim reached his tether's end
And vetoed compromises
Judge Jeffreys was let loose with black cap and a noose
The, oh so, Bloody Assizes [10]

Now some of Jim's screws went missing
It's not clear what he'd got
Lacking confidence and making no blinking sense
He'd completely lost the plot! [11]

Protestants, wanting him out
Sought help across the water
Where William of Orange who doesn't rhyme with anything
Had wed Mary, Jim's eldest daughter

William quite fancied a Kingdom;
Mary never liked Dad that much
So over they came, for power and fame
To kick him into touch

Jim, who'd got wind they were coming
Felt sure he could beat them – until
His Protestant men deserted; and then
Went and joined forces with Will! [12]

This wasn't his final defeat
At the Boyne he had a last chance [13]
Just for a while he ruled The Emerald Isle
Till Will sent him packing, to France

The Irish thought him a coward
When he did a moonlight flit
And instead of James used other rude names [14]
Notably "Seamus The ... bodily function"

Jim's body was exhumed [15]
And scattered near and far
Except his brain which still remains
In Paris, in a jar [16]

Stuff about James II

1. He was in fact "James II of England and VII of Scotland" (and indeed King of Ireland (iv)), so having already had a "Jim 1/6 [d]" we must now endure a "...2/7 [d]. (Ed.)

2. Not only was he the second son of Charles I and brother of Charles II, both arguably "scary" enough anyway, he was also a Catholic, and that was really scary at that time. (Ed.)

3. David Hilliam, for example, describes James as being "... just as lecherous as his brother Charles ..." (i)

4. Two years after his father, Charles I, lost Oxford James fled to Holland (1648) where he fought with both armies. (ii)

5. He was promoted Lord High Admiral, later to resign as a result of the anti Catholic Test Act of 1673; he was finally re-appointed in 1684. (ii)

6. New Amsterdam, a Dutch possession, fell in 1665, to become New York upon its presentation by Charles II to his brother, later to be James II, who was then Duke of York. (ii)

7. James married Anne Hyde in 1660 but she died and he married Mary Beatrice of Modena (no, she did not found the Ferrari factory (Ed.)) in 1673. (ii) She threatened to enter a nunnery if he did not give up his "perpetual sex with other women". (i)

8. See "Stuff 9"

9. There are whole books to be read here but, in brief, James kept dissolving Parliament, Bills were produced to "exclude" Catholics but defeated; James wanted a more "biddable" parliament; there were risings leading to the Glorious Revolution of 1688 -9 and the appearance of the Protestant William of Orange, later to become King with Mary, his cousin, James II's daughter. (ii)

10. Chief Justice Judge Jeffreys sentenced 300 to death in the summer of 1685 after Monmouth, an illegitimate, but Protestant, son of Charles II failed to overthrow James. (ii) Even so the Assizes became much more infamous later because at the time "... rows of gibbets were nothing special in the political culture". (iii)

11. "James' later years were clouded by morose religiosity." (ii)

12. James fled London in November 1688 when William invaded but on recapture in December he was taken to London where William persuaded him to go to France. (ii)

13. James returned from his court in exile in France to Ireland but was again defeated, at the Battle of The Boyne, and returned again to France where he died. (v)

14. After his defeat James did not stay in Dublin, but rode with a small escort to Duncannon and returned to exile in France, even though his army left the field relatively unscathed. James's loss of nerve and speedy exit from the battlefield enraged his Irish supporters, who

fought on until the Treaty of Limerick in 1691; he was derisively nicknamed Seamus a' chaca ("James the shit") in Irish. (iv)

15. He was originally buried at Germain-en-Laye. (iv)
16. The brain' receptacle is actually "… a bronze urn in a chapel at The Scots College in Paris".(i)

More Stuff about James II

(i)   Hilliam, David; Kings, Queens, Bones and Bastards; Sutton; Gloucestershire, England; 2001 (printed by J Haynes of Sparkford who also do car workshop manuals, by the way)
(ii) Gardiner, Juliet and Wenborn, N, Eds; The History Today Companion to British History; Collins and Brown; London; 1995.
(iii) Schama, S ;A History of Britain (1603 – 1776); BBC Worldwide Limited; London; 2000;
(iv) www. Newworldencyclopedia (sic).org/entry/ James_II_of_England;
(v)   www.en.wikipedia.org/wiki/Battle_of_the_Boyne;

WILLIAM (III) AND MARY (II)
"The Oranges"

(William 1650-1702)
(Mary 1662 – 1694)

(co-regency 1692 – 1694) [1]

(William r. 1694 – 1702)

England had been lacking zest
This couple found a solution
Their time on the throne has since been known
As "The Glorious Revolution" [2]

The Oranges were cordially welcomed
As soon as Jim sounded retreat
Were they England's cure? – No one could be sure
Truth is, they had little to beat [3]

Few tears were shed for Jim
Folk were full of good cheer
He'd a good many flaws and his Catholic cause
Was a ruddy great flop over here

So! – First a Bill of Rights [4]
Triumphantly laid down
This was heaven sent for Parliament
The People and the Crown

Their victory won, they'd much to do
To honour the people's trust
Their confidence growing and cups overflowing
They slept the sleep of the just

Next day, after a lie in
They rose to find aids in a flap
It was a bit of a groan, there was only one throne
For months she'd to sit on his lap!

Two heads to put together
Less chance to disappoint
Uniquely rare this wedded pair!
The only time Monarchs were joint

So were they a match made in heaven?
When she met him, was she best pleased?
In fact, she thought him base and loathed his face [5]
To her, it looked freshly squeezed!

Their love didn't easily blossom
Her servant was his lover [6]
But they learned to gel and rub along pretty well
With a healthy respect for each other

They had duties both sides of the Channel
And had to work out where they went
She stayed over here for most of the year
While he was in-continent

A wise woman was Mary
She ruled with guile and sense [7]
Whilst he was at pains to fight his campaigns
Always at great expense [8]

Parliament, who had the clout
Passed the Tonnage Act
And The Bank of England was duly devised [9]
To provide the money they lacked

Everyone loved good-natured Mary
And she loved them in return
The same could not be said for Bill, who instead
Was cold, silent and stern

Hence a lack of kiddies
They weren't in the grand design
Pity, 'cos here's a nice thing, an Orange offspring
Could be "Pip" or "Clementine"

Mary had but a short innings
The Grim Reaper found her at home
The smallpox he gave her meant nothing could save her
Bill had to go it alone

Without his bride beside him
(This was not foreseen!)
For a change perhaps he courted chaps [10]
Now he was King and Queen!

For eight years as "King Bill"
He ruled alone … until
While out hunting one day, his horse turned the wrong way
And tripped on a giant molehill!

The result of which was mixed
Some bad news and some rather lovely
Not good for Bill, he became gravely ill
But the horse made a full recovery

Bill's life was held on amber
His physician scratched his head
He didn't know where to begin – complications set in
And the orange light turned to red [11]

Stuff about William and Mary

1. Although the reign was, at first, a co-regency, research has revealed little attributable solely to Mary, apart from, importantly, her popularity. (Ed.)
2. The "Glorious Revolution" is the name traditionally given to the sequence of events, in 1688 and 1699, involving the continuing antipathy between Protestants and Catholics, culminating in an invitation to William of Orange to invade. (i) Strictly speaking, therefore, this preceded "their time on the throne". (Ed.)
3. William and Mary certainly had "little to beat" in following James II who was "… inept and tactless" and unique as the only King of England "… driven from the kingdom …" and dying in exile; The worst of his "… many faults …" in most people's eyes was that of being a Catholic". (ii)
4. The Bill of Rights included the importance of Parliament and The People but, crucially, forbade Catholic succession to the throne. (i)
5. Whether it was appearance ("… slightly hunchbacked …" and "… shorter …" (ii)), the age difference (at the time of the marriage she was 15, he 26) or the fact that he was a cousin (unlikely given the mores of the time (Ed.), she was certainly unhappy and cried for days before and "… even … during …" the wedding. (ii)
6. Her servant, Elizabeth Villiers, a childhood friend of William, became his mistress. (ii)
7. Mary was in fact, if not in William's eyes, next in line to the throne and, during William's frequent absences, in control. (Ed.)
8. William frequently involved England in his wars, and their not inconsiderable cost, against his traditional enemy, The French. (iv)
9. The Tonnage Act of 1694 was designed to raise funds, by subscription, for ships to fight the French, and the Bank of England was founded to hold those funds. (iii)
10. Some argue that William was homosexual but that may have been a spurious argument, including about his relationship with William Bentinck, a former page, put forward by his Jacobite (followers of James) enemies. (iv)
11. William's death was attributable to a mole, hence the Jacobite toast to "… the little gentleman in the velvet overcoat …". William is interred in Westminster Abbey, without a memorial. (iv)

More Stuff about William and Mary

(i) Gardiner, Juliet, Ed; The History Today Companion to British History; Collins and Brown; London; 1995.

(ii) Hilliam, David; Kings, Queens, Bones and Bastards; Sutton; Gloucestershire, England; 2001

(iii) http://www.bankofengland.co.uk/about/Documents/legislation/1694act.pdf;

(iv) http://en.wikipedia.org/wiki/William_III_of_England

QUEEN ANNE
"Anne with an 'e' "

(1665 – 1714)
(r.1702 – 1714)

After Willie's untimely demise
(He'd cracked his nut on a tree)
It's time to explore his sister-in-law [1]
His successor, Anne with an 'e'

***

Now, hold this mental image
She's rather squat and frumpy
We know from her chairs that her legs had no hairs
And were ornate, bowed and stumpy [2]

Anne wed George, a Danish Prince [3]
To ensure heirs aplenty
But although they strived none survived
Not one, of almost twenty! [4]

But Anne and George still flourished
And got along a treat
And for close support she appointed her Consort
Admiral of The Fleet [5]

Monarchs who legislated
Had reached their final hour
No longer needed – they'd been superseded
By ministerial power [6]

With a final regal flourish
Copyright Law began [7]
A last Royal vote to protect those who wrote
Was known as "The Statute of Anne"

It was a Golden Age for Literature
For quills and ink to flow
The timeless gifts of Pope and Swift
And, of course, Defoe [8]

In Parliament's ring stood two giants
Fighting dirty and telling tall stores
The red corner prigs were known as The Whigs [9]
The blue, like now, were The Tories [10]

Notably, during Anne's reign
The first Act of Union was written [11]
Now England and Scotland would go hand in hand
Under the name "Great Britain"

This Queen liked a bosom pal
Sarah Churchill the first she chose [12]
But power pollutes, Sal got big for her boots
This got right up Anne's nose!

Her next close buddy was Abigail Hill [13]
A plant of the artful Tories
Abby's routine was to influence The Queen
With politically biased stories

To meddle with Spanish Succession [14]
The Duke of Marlborough set sail [15]
A man august, and one she could trust
Most likely to prevail

Anne hoped he'd do better than Raleigh
Who'd fought many a campaign
His purloined goods were something called spuds
And tobacco that fuddles the brain

The Duke was quick to assure her
"I've had more success than Walter
I knew the truth that you have a sweet tooth,
So I got you some rock – called Gibraltar"

If she'd only known the truth
She'd have created a helluva stink
But I'm pleased to report that she always thought
Gibraltar was sweet … and pink

The Treaty of Utrecht [16]
Made the Spanish wince
It broke the deadlock to cede us their rock
But they've fussed about it since

That a blood disorder took her [17]
Was no great catastrophe
And the cannons fired for Reign – Uninspired
And the end of Anne with an 'e'

Of the symptoms of her illness
You may not be aware
I can confide that she grew so wide
Her coffin was all but square! [18]

Stuff about Anne

1. Anne was the sister of Mary, wife of the previous monarch, William. (i)
2. Everyone except the author knows that "Queen Anne Legs" refers to the style of furniture at the time of her reign – not her own legs! (Ed.)
3. Anne married a staunch Protestant, Prince George of Denmark in 1683. (ii)
4. Many of her 17 pregnancies were abortive and no child survived to adulthood. (iii)
5. Anne awarded her husband George, Prince of Denmark, the (largely honorary) title of Lord High Admiral in 1702. (iii) Queen Elizabeth II awarded that title to her husband, The Duke of Edinburgh, on his 90th birthday in 2011 (iv)
6. Anyone following these "poems" anything like chronologically will have witnessed the gradual dilution of the monarch's power. (Ed.)
7. The Copyright Act was first passed in England in 1709. (v)
8. Daniel Defoe 1661[?] – 1731, much involved in "politics"; Alexander Pope 1688 1744 a poet and a Roman Catholic; Jonathan Swift 1667 – 1745 an Irishman who at first supported the Whigs then the Tories. (vi)
9. Much has been written to explain "The Whigs" but one quote is particularly apt: "They presented themselves as archetypal merchants, their critics represented them as archetypal speculators and profiteers." There were of course complex religious affinities too. (vii)
10. The term "Tories" comes from the Irish Toraidhe (bandit cattle thief etc.) and was used as an insult to these politicians who comprised many landowners (caricatured as backwoods squires), merchants and lawyers. (vii)
11. The Act of Union of 1707 united England and Scotland but Ireland was not included until the similar Act of 1801. (v)
12. Sarah Churchill (née Jennings) was at first a servant, then a confidante and close friend, of Anne, but as she became increasingly active, with Whig leanings, so she fell out of favour with the Queen. (ii)
13. Abigail Hill had once been a servant of Sarah Churchill (see Stuff 11), a niece of Abigail's mother, but being much more a Tory, than a Whig, as was Anne, "took over" Sarah Churchill's favoured position. But she too began to try to be increasingly influential, pressing the Tory cause. (viii)
14. The War of Spanish Succession lasted, on and off, from 1702 to 1713 and was essentially fought over the distribution of the Spanish dominions after the death of the last Hapsburg King of Spain, Charles II, in 1700. (vii)
15. The Duke of Marlborough, or John Churchill, 1650 -1722, was the husband of Sarah (see "Stuff 11" and elsewhere) and a prominent

military leader under William (of Orange) rising to commander of all allied forces (largely against France) under Anne but lost power and went into voluntary exile when the Tories gained the upper hand. Winston Churchill was a descendant and the "grandiose" Blenheim palace was named after Marlborough's first major victory. (ii)

16. The Treaty (or "Peace") of Utrecht in 1713 ended the War of Spanish Succession and ceded Gibraltar to Britain but in order to get it passed Anne had to appoint a largely Tory Ministry. (ii) and (vii)

17. Anne's increasing ill health kept the issue of the succession to the fore. (ii)

18. It is said that Anne died of a cerebral haemorrhage and became so fat with "dropsy" and gluttony, that her coffin was almost square. (ix) She lies in Westminster Abbey, where she is surrounded by 16 stillborn children and one who survived 11 years. (x)

More Stuff about Anne

(i) Family Tree of the British Monarchy; Encyclopaedia Britannica, 15th Edition 1994

(ii) (ii) Gardiner, Juliet, Ed; The History Today Who's Who in British History; Collins and Brown; London; 2000

(iii) http://en.wikipedia.org/wiki/List_of_Lord_High_Admirals_and_First_ Lords_of_the_Ad miralty;

(iv) http://www.telegraph.co.uk/news/uknews/prince-philip/8568387/Queen-makes-Dukeof-Edinburgh-head-of-the-Navy-as-90th-birthday-gift.html;

(v) Bailie, J. M. (no relation); General Ed; Hamlyn Dictionary of Dates and Anniversaries; Book Club Associates; London; 1978

(vi) Various Eds. (esp. Oxbury, H.F.); The Concise Dictionary of National Biography; The Softback Preview and The Oxford University Press; (OUP 1992; Oxford)

(vii) Gardiner, Juliet and Wenborn, N., Eds; The History Today Companion to British History; Collins and Brown; London; 1995

(viii) (http://en.wikipedia.org/wiki/Abigail_Masham,_Baroness_Masham)

(ix) Hilliam, David; Kings, Queens, Bones and Bastards; Sutton; Gloucestershire, England; 2001

(x) Kerrigan, M; Who Lies Where; Fourth Estate; London 1995

C. Díaz

George I
"German George"

(1660 – 1727)
(r.1714 – 1727)

The passing of "Anne with an 'e' "
Brought The Stuarts to a close
The next decision caused bitter division
George, the Herr they chose [1]

He'd been given a nice English name [2]
That was merely by chance
With slightly less luck we could have been stuck
With King Wolfgang, Helmut or Hans!

But Protestants would have anyone
Who'd keep their faith alive
George was repressed and way past his best
At almost fifty-five

Dissenters (of whom there were many)
Were determined not to roll over
Tories and Jacobites fought for Catholic rights [3]
And spurned this King from Hanover

Sophia, his wife (and cousin)
Strayed with a handsome Swede [4]
But before her fun she'd born him a son [5]
The next George to succeed

So! ... A life in jail for Sophia [6]
George couldn't forgive her
And a watery end for The Count, her friend
Face down in a river! [7]

George arrived with mistresses
Who became a laughing stock
Charlotte, the first, looked a lot like a bratwurst
The other a rake in a frock [8]

George was slow to adapt
With arrogance quite spectacular
British culture he spurned and only learned
The basics of our vernacular [9]

Outwardly distant and dull
And hardly ever seen out!
Cynical, sardonic … Far too Teutonic!
He was just an old sauerkraut

That the British chose to hate him
He fancied most unfair
So he kept up the pad where he'd lived as a lad [10]
And spent some of his time over there

But was George implicated
In some economic trouble
When to great personal cost large fortunes were lost
Known as 'The South Sea Bubble'? [11]

"Ich k'no zee Britishers hate me"; said he
"Zay sink me crude and sinister
Veel need a man to take charge ven I'm nicht at large
Und vee'll call him….zee 'Pry Minister' " [12]

The head of the Whigs was Rob Walpole
This man was nobody's mug!
He was bright and abrupt but proven corrupt
For which he'd done time in jug [13]

George stood back and dithered
Walpole got on with the job
And what became plain was by the end of his reign
The real power lay with Rob!

Now credit where it's due
George helped with treaties and laws
That helped to arrange that for a nice change
We avoided fruitless wars

So, George wasn't fond of England
And made that very plain
In seventeen twenty seven he was re-routed to heaven [14]
And didn't have to come here again

Stuff about George I

1. Although the late Queen Anne had over 50 relatives closer than George they were all Catholics so banned from the throne by The Act of Settlement 1701. (i)
2. Well, actually he was in fact "Georg (with a hard "G") Ludwig", Anglicised later to "George Louis". (Ed.)
3. See also "Stuff 1" (Ed.)
4. He was Philip Christoph von Königsmarck. (Ed.)
5. The son with George was Georg August, later George II. (ii)
6. Sophia spent the last 30 years of her life imprisoned, by George, in Ahlen Castle. She died there in 1726, aged 60. (iii)
7. Possibly Die Leine in Germany (iv)
8. This is a reference to Melusine von der Schulenburg who became a go between for ministers unwilling to approach George directly. George and Melusine (tall and thin and known as "The Maypole") had three daughters but the paternity was never admitted and they were treated as Melusine's nieces. (ii) Also to the enormously fat Sophia von Kilmansegg, known as "The Elephant", who also accompanied George to England on his accession. (v)
9. George's English was certainly limited but he did speak French (the language of political business) as well as German, Latin and some Dutch and Italian. (ii)
10. George spent much time at the Herrenhausen in Hanover (he was Elector [in effect "ruler" or "king" of the Electorate, or area (Ed.)]. of Hanover) although "London was his main base for politics". (ii)
11. The South Sea Company was essentially a vehicle through which the government could borrow more cheaply than through its own bonds. When the bubble burst in 1721 many people lost very heavily, financiers fled or killed themselves. (vi) The fact that the King himself was a primary loser may have allowed him to escape personal blame. (Ed.)
12. Walpole became First Lord of the Treasury in 1721, effectively "Prime Minister" Although the South Sea Bubble (see "Stuff 13") had just burst he appeared exonerated as he held no office (other than "Inmate of The Tower") when the scheme had been put into action in 1712. (ii)
13. He spent time in The Tower of London after losing office and being involved in corruption scandals in 1712. (ii)
14. The superstitious George had been told by a fortune teller that he would die within a year of his imprisoned wife. She died in 1726 and in 1727, on his way to Germany (having bid his son and daughter-in-law farewell "for ever"), he had a stroke and died in Osnabruck. He was originally buried in a church in Hanover then, after WWII, reburied at Herrenhausen. (vii)

More Stuff about George I

(i)   http://en.wikipedia.org/wiki/George_I_of_Great_Britain
(ii) Gardiner, Juliet, Ed; The History Today Who's Who in British History; Collins and Brown; London; 2000
(iii) http://en.wikipedia.org/wiki/Sophia_Dorothea_of_Celle
(iv) http://en.wikipedia.org/wiki/Philip_Christoph_von_K%C3%B6nigsmarck
(v)   Hilliam, David; Kings, Queens, Bones and Bastards; Sutton; Gloucestershire, England; 2001
(vi) Gardiner, Juliet and Wenborn, N., Eds; The History Today Companion to British History; Collins and Brown; London; 1995
(vii) Kerrigan, M; Who Lies Where; Fourth Estate; London 1995

C. Díaz

GEORGE II
Soldier George [1]

(1683–1760)
(r.1727-1760)

When the German bloke had his stroke
They had to run some checks
Most everyone was glad he'd gone
But who the heck was next?

Catholics had a golden chance
To champion their contender
Know then, and since, as "The Bonnie Prince" [2]
Charlie – The Young Pretender

People must have had their doubts;
Was it clever to depend?
On the adequacy of a Charlie
Who was likely to pretend!

With power held by Protestants
Catholics stood no chance
So in was beckoned George the Second
While Charlie stewed in France

This George had loathed his father [3]
Who was frosty and unkind
When told he was dead, he just yawned and said;
"Oh dear, what a pity; never mind!"

He'd been bursting for his go
Lurking like a vulture
He'd lived over here, enjoyed warm beer
And swore by English culture

He's a man whose moods would swing
An often troubled soul
In a fit of pique he had a really mean streak [4]
And could really lose control!

George had four inspirations
He cherished them all his life
The armed forces, music and horses
And Caroline, his wife

Eight kids his soul mate bore him
Her cup was full to the brim
She was sober of thought and breathed life into Court [5]
(How did she fit all that in?)

Because of his love for this lady
You'd think he'd have played on the level
No! – As regards fluff, George could not get enough [6]
He was a right little devil!

One of two traits he got from his dad
The other a musical ear
A concerto recital was thrilling and vital
To keep them both in good cheer

Their favourite 'turn' was Handel
Some wonderful music he'd make
His tunes and writing were so exciting
Some people stayed awake! [7]

Now, what of the Bonnie Prince?
Whose claim had been in vain
His hopes revived in seventeen forty five
When he tried for the Throne again

Defeat, though, at Culloden [8]
Scuppered his kingly plans
The last bloody toil on British soil
Not counting football fans!

Robert Walpole was still PM
Caroline, his fierce supporter
Rob wanted to rent close to Parliament
Which he leaked to a passing reporter

"He needs a place in London", said Caroline
"Near work to save wear on his feet
In Hing Street, on the right is a bijou campsite
His address'll be "Tent down Hing Street" [9]

190

We'd not had a war for ages
George loved them and wanted a treat
So we started again, this time with Spain [10]
Who were as easy as heck to beat

Soon after he picked on France [11]
And, of course, the Dutch
Winning a war made his status soar
Both were an easy touch

This King had a deal of bravery [12]
He'd much sooner die than yield
No monarch since then has led men
On a gory battlefield

When you conjure a mental image
Imagine him right off his head
Threatening, blaspheming, complaining and screaming
Royals were so interbred!

On the other throne one day [13]
His life went down the pan
Fred, his son, had already gone [14]
Make way for a gaga man! [15]

Stuff about George II

1. The sobriquet "Soldier George" alludes to his fondness, first shown during his education in "Germany", for military matters (Ed.) He had been allowed to command a unit in The War of Spanish Succession (c. 1708). (ii)

2. The Catholics still hoped for a Catholic ruler, this time Charles Edward Stewart, "The Young Pretender" or "Bonnie Prince Charlie", son of "The Old Pretender" who in turn was the son of the exiled Stuart King, James II & VII. (See also earlier poem). (i)

3. There was little love lost between father and son, the then Prince George established a rival court at Leicester House (as indeed did his own son, Frederick, in 1737) although there had been something of a reconciliation in 1720 after which, for a few years, Prince George remained on the political sidelines. (ii)

4. "Opinionated and assertive" [a euphemism?] "George was always a force to be reckoned with". (ii)

5. Caroline, a supporter of Walpole, used her "charm and good sense" to guide the "King's early dealings with politicians". (ii)

6. Perhaps temporibus aliter, perhaps not! (Ed.) Certainly "Caroline accepted without fuss [his English mistress] Mrs. Howard" and his grandmother said "... at least it might improve his English". (ii) On George's death "hundreds of locks of women's hair were discovered among his personal belongings". (iii)

7. Handel (1685 – 1759), had settled in England during the reign of George I, who, as Elector of Hanover, had earlier appointed him Kapellmeister, (ii) and father and son each enjoyed his music, (iii) even if the author of these verses, Philistinian soccer loving fan that he is, does not. (Ed.)

8. Charles' defeat at Culloden in 1745, following which he fled to France, and very many of his wounded were massacred by "The Butcher" Duke of Cumberland, was an effective end to the Jacobite claims. (iv)

9. Whilst Walpole was indeed the first PM in 10 Downing Street and there is a "Hing Street" it is, unfortunately, in Hong Kong, not London. So this verse is all ... let us say "poetic licence". Give me strength! (Ed.)

10. The so called "War of Jenkins' Ear" (1739 – 1748) (a name relating to the severed (allegedly by Spanish coastguards) ear of the captain of a British merchant ship. (v)

11. The War of Jenkins' Ear became subsumed in the later Europe wide War of Austrian Succession, which, some thought, had more to do with George's Hanoverian interests than his British ones; it involved, amongst others, France and The Netherlands. (ii)

12. The Battle of Dettingen in 1742 was the last time a reigning British Monarch commanded in battle. (ii)
13. George II had a heart attack while sitting on a lavatory. (iii)
14. George's son, Frederick, had died in 1751, leaving his son to become George III. The cause of his death is uncertain, but may have been attributable to a cricket or real tennis accident. (vi)
15. Much has been said of "The Madness of King George" and more will follow in the next poem. (Ed.)

More Stuff about George II

(i)   http://en.wikipedia.org/wiki/Charles_Edward_Stuart
(ii) Gardiner, Juliet, Ed; The History Today Who's Who in British History; Collins and Brown; London; 2000
(iii) Hilliam, David; Kings, Queens, Bones and Bastards; Sutton; Gloucestershire, England; 2001
(iv) Gardiner, Juliet, and Wenborn, Neil, Eds; The History Today Companion to British History; Collins and Brown; London; 1995
(v)   http://en.wikipedia.org/wiki/War_of_Jenkins%27_Ear
(vi) http://en.wikipedia.org/wiki/Frederick,_Prince_of_Wales#Cricket

C. Díaz

GEORGE III
"Bark-King George"

(1738 – 1820)
(r.1738 – 1820)

George the Second's eldest lad
Went by the name of Freddie
Sadly he'd gone, making way for his son
Who plainly wasn't ready

This George was close to his parents
But his grandpa and he didn't click [1]
He was listless, hazy and often plain lazy
Which came across as thick

What he lacked in brains and belief
He made up for with self-will and guile
It was a curious blend, which would often offend
A most individual style!

He had bursts of mad behaviour
Naturally causing alarm
Would he take the helm of this powerful realm?
Or live on a funny farm!

Not until his wedding day
Did he meet with Charlotte, his wife [2]
So, no prior inspection but a deep affection
She was the love of his life

She baked him fifteen buns
"Give me heirs" he had said
With all that baking (not to mention the making)
She could hardly have got out of bed

A Prime Minister who he could bully
This to George was a must
The choice was enough but, like now, it was tough
To find a bloke you could trust

Three total washouts, he had
Then far better luck with the fourth
A man who could be led to do as George said
He was Frederick, Lord North [3]

Together they made a plan
Send troops to the USA
In coats of red young blood was shed [4]
Truly a darkest day! [5]

After that he'd other PM's
"They're all the pits" was his claim
They knew what he meant and as if to consent
Two even had Pitt as their name [6]

George suffered a total breakdown
Foaming mouth and faraway stare
Though it cost a packet he'd a nice new straight jacket
And straps on a specially built chair

Mustard poultices stuck on his body
To cure his tragic malaise
By drawing out evil humours?
They'd some daft ideas in those days!

Too soon to write him off
His wits returned a year later
Back to demonstrate that though Britain was Great
He could make it even greater

Once again we'd sort out the French
Who behaved like big ugly brutes
That Bonaparte, the jumped-up little f ... Frenchman
Was far too big for his boots [7]

George sent word to Lord Nelson
(Who was named after a pub in Nuneaton) [8]
"Engage the small French prat in a funny shaped hat
And give him a jolly good beating

"That garlic eater's a danger"; said Horatio
"I've heard that when he's about
One whiff of his breath'll condemn you to death
So I'll keep a watchful eye out"

"And what if I fall in battle"; he asked
Said George, "Yes, that would be a pity
But don't look so solemn, you'll be stuck on a column [9]
With a panoramic view of the city"

(We all know by now
That this was an armless deception
They couldn't solve how to make it revolve
So he just looks in one direction)

The King's illness caused violent mood swings
From rage to deep melancholy
It scrambled his mind and sent him blind
He ended up right off his trolley

His son took over as captain
Taking the helm of the nation
As The Prince of Wales he kept wind in our sails
Right up 'til his own coronation

George had a pitiful ending
Deaf, blind and mad in his grief
After ten long years of frustration and tears
Death was a blessed relief

Stuff about George III

1. George II was his grandfather, his father Frederick died when George (later III) was 12. George III was the first Hanoverian King of England born and bred in Britain and was brought up by his mother and various tutors; he went to Cambridge at 14. (i)
2. George married Charlotte Mecklenburg Strelitz in 1761 and was devoted both to her and to their fifteen children. (i)
3. Frederick North was known as "Lord North" even before his elevation late in life. His father was a courtier to Frederick Prince of Wales (George's father): Lord North resembled George III and contemporary rumours held that The Prince of Wales was his father too. Although usually acquiescing to George III's wishes North did resign forcing The King to accede to the American wishes, thus ending the War of Independence. (i)
4. British Infantrymen (the musket carrying "Redcoats") wore red coats in battle from the start of the Seven Years War in 1756 and for about another century.(v)
5. The loss of the American Colonies after the War of American Independence (1775 – 1783); troubles at home, and declarations of war from the French, the Spanish, and the Dutch led George to consider abdication. (i) & (ii)
6. William Pitt the Elder (1708 – 1778) and his son William Pitt the Younger (1759-1808) each served as Prime Minister during George's reign. When William Pitt the Younger first became P.M., aged 24, (Britain's youngest ever Prime Minister) late in 1783, his administration was known as the "mince pie administration" as people expected it to be gone by Christmas: it was not. (i)
7. Although Napoleon was to rise again, Nelson's defeat of the Franco-Spanish fleet at Trafalgar (during which Nelson fell, fatally struck by a sniper's bullet) was decisive and gave Britain naval supremacy for the next 100 years. (ii)
8. Not an uncommon pub name throughout England, where there are 78 of them (and a few in Sydney Australia (Ed.)) but, perhaps surprisingly, not in the 50 most common. (iii)
9. Nelson's Column was built between 1840 and 1843 at a cost of £47,000 and re-furbished in 2006 for £420,000 and was found to be 4.4 m shorter than previously supposed, being 51.6m from the bottom of the pedestal to the top of Nelson's hat. (iv)

More Stuff about George III

(i)   Gardiner, Juliet, Ed; The History Today Who's Who in British History; Collins and Brown; London; 2000.
(ii) Gardiner, Juliet and Wenborn, N, Eds; The History Today Companion to British History; Collins and Brown; London; 1995.
(iii) http://www.dailymail.co.uk/home/moslive/article-1374494/Red-Lion-White-Hart-Mostpopular-pub-names-England.html
(iv) http://en.wikipedia.org/wiki/Nelson's_Column
(v)   Holmes, Richard; Redcoat; HarperCollins; London; 2001

GEORGE IV
The Prince Regent [1] "Randy" [2]

(1762 – 1830)
(r.1820-1830) [3]

George's One and Two
Both through the door
And three has gone … whereupon
Let's meet number four

It's not easy being a Monarch [4]
There's a heck of a lot to know
But in the case of Randy what came in handy
Was his time being de facto

Which meant, like his name "Prince Regent"
(Terms you may have missed)
That he'd a sworn obligation to lead the Nation
While his dad was round the twist

Inebriate in his teens
This was a carefree soul
His money was frittered and he freely admitted
To be totally out of control [5]

Bark-King had no time for Randy [6]
The reverse was also the position
You see, father son hate was a family trait [7]
And they proudly upheld the tradition

His dad said: "I despair of your bad habits
And your attitude's most unpleasant!
You'll be sad when you've sent me mad"
But when he had – he wasn't

Randy fell for the Fitzherbert's daughter
A stunner called Maria
When Bark-King learns he has one of his turns
Forbidding him to see her

201

She was Catholic and already wed [8]
A flighty little bit
Still George smothered her with kisses and made her his missus
Ignoring the daft old twit

So, did they live happily ever after?
Did his heart overrule his dad's head?
Tragically no – Maria had to go
He'd to marry his cousin instead

Her name was "Caroline of Brunswick" [9]
She loathed him – but he loathed her more
He treated her bitterly so she lived in Italy
With a baby girl she'd bore

Politicians had now concluded
That a sleeping monarch was best
And that the very best thing about this here King
Was his lack of interest [10]

George passionately loved the arts [11]
He bought paintings, fine lace and Ming
He was civilized, cultured and wise
Not just a philandering King

He told his mate, architect John Nash [12]
"I've got big plans for London, old chum [13]
And if we do it well, who can tell
We might get tourists to come!"

We need somewhere for exotic animals
Like Noah had his Ark
There's some land that'll do where we'll build a zoo
We'll call that "Regent's Park" [14]

Then a nice long road with shops
Where the Yanks and Japs can meet
Wide, for when we have cars – lots of burger bars
We'll call that "Regent Street"

And then, of course, there's fashion
I want everything named after me
Buildings, windows and gables – furniture, chairs and tables
That'll all be called "Regency"

Randy was an enigma
Variations complexly embroiled
Fun and disarming, witty and charming
But also lazy and spoiled

So fat was George in later life
He broke the Royal scales
And the people would cry as he passed by
"There goes The Prince of Whales!" [15]

He checked out in Eighteen Thirty
Not stopping to settle the bill [16]
But his artefacts remain intact
So we can enjoy them still

Stuff about George IV

1. Better known as "The Prince Regent" perhaps, for his time as "Prince Regent" during his father's incapacity" (1811 – 1820) than as King George IV. Despite the opening verse, referring to George III "... had gone ..." much of this poem deals with the Regency. (i)
2. George is also referred to by our illustrious author as "Randy" (for reasons which will become apparent, including the fact that when he married Caroline (see "Stuff 10") ... he had a vast range of delectable mistresses ...). (iii)
3. He was also King of Ireland, and King of Hanover. (i)
4. But possibly easier than "Bein' Green". (ii)
5. His sex life and drinking orgies were the scandal of his time" (iii)
6. The derivation of the word "Barking" to mean "mad" is more likely attributable to the barking of mad dogs than the mental asylum in that part of London. (iv)
7. "Like most of the Hanoverians ..." (i)
8. George married "Mrs Fitzherbert" who had been (twice) widowed and so debarred from marriage to the heir to the British Throne without the King's consent (Royal Marriages Act 1772) which was refused. Moreover, she was from an old Catholic family so even if valid the marriage would have excluded George from succession to the throne under the terms of the Act of Settlement 1701. (v)
9. The marriage was unsuccessful as soon as George saw what turned out to be a very unattractive, rotten toothed, smelly, woman. (iii)
10. For example, "... when the Prime Minister Lord Liverpool fell ill in 1827, George at one stage suggested that ministers should choose Liverpool's successor". (vi)
11. Many of the paintings which he acquired now hang in the "Royal Collection". (Ed.)
12. John Nash (1752 – 1835) also played a large part in the design and layout of Trafalgar Square and St. James' Park. (i)
13. Not only London, but Brighton too where George built the "... dome and minaret-encrusted pavilion for Mrs. Fitzherbert. " (i)
14. This, and the architectural references that follow (plus the Nash designed enlargement of Buckingham Palace and The Mall) are well known landmarks (and tourist attractions) and require no further comment. (Ed.)
15. The young dandy had, in later life, become obese, and was known as "The Prince of Whales" in some circles. (i)
16. Known for his extravagance throughout his life there is no evidence that his projects were ever self-funding. (Ed.)

More Stuff about George IV

(i)   Gardiner, Juliet, Ed; The History Today Who's Who in British History; Collins and Brown; London; 2000.

(ii)   http://en.wikipedia.org/wiki/Brin'_Green

(iii) Hilliam, David; Kings, Queens, Bones and Bastards; Sutton; Gloucestershire, England; 2001

(iv) http://www.phrases.org.uk/meanings/barking-mad.html;

(v)   http://en.wikipedia.org/wiki/Royal_Marriages_Act_1772

(vi) http://www.royal.gov.uk/historyofthemonarchy/ kingsandqueensoftheunitedkingdom/thehanoverians/georgeiv.aspx

C. Díaz

WILLIAM IV
"Silly Billy" [1]

(1765 – 1837)
(r.1830 -1837)

As Randy exits, stage left
Who's waiting in the wing?
With no kids on show it's left to his bro
Billy, a sailor king [2]

Rum swigging, climbing the rigging
Endlessly tying sheepshanks
Long and short trips on dozens of ships
Making his way through the ranks

Finally reaching the top
Admiral of the Fleet [3]
The best man, you think? – Or a nod and a wink
It helps to be elite

A kindly, warm-hearted man
With charm and bon ami
Eccentric enough, loud mouthed and bluff
Due to his time at sea

The love of his life was an actress
Dorothy Jordan by name [4]
They'd ten offspring – that's a hell of a fling!
None had a Royal claim

He knew his Kingship would come into dock
So had to dump poor Dot
A queen must be Royal and, for preference, unsoiled
Dot was most certainly not!

She made way for Adelaide [5]
Their kids would fit the bill
There were, in fact, two, but neither pulled through
Children twelve – heirs nil!

Willie was an uninspired man
Never a king at heart
He'd no purpose or drive and at sixty-five
He'd no great desire to start

Parliamentary reform was in order
Bills were duly floated
Many matters of state, but the crucial debate
Was simply how they voted [6]

His politically biased decisions
Taken and recanted
Of his meddlesome ways and ham interplays
People were disenchanted

Billy was the last Monarch
Who'd try to be political [7]
And although Parliament still needs Royal Assent
Now the Ruler can't be critical.

In the June of thirty seven
Pneumonia struck without warning
What a bummer – damned English Summer
Let's blame global warming!

His eulogy was short on esteem
At its tail a critical sting
"Though past his peak, ignorant and weak
He was honest – for a King!" [8]

Stuff about William IV

1. William IV was "... abrupt and outspoken, irascible though basically good-natured, unpredictable and eccentric, he was called the original 'Silly Billy' " (i)
2. He joined the Royal Navy in 1779 aged 14. (ii)
3. This appointment was made in 1811, followed by Lord High Admiral 16 years later. (ii)
4. He lived with her from 1790 to 1811 (ii) (but despite verse 2, line 2, never tied that particular knot. (Ed.)
5. His marriage (many hands had been sought but declined until Princess Adelaide of Saxe Meiningen accepted) was not until 1818. Meanwhile William had been "desperately in love" with an English heiress, Miss Wykham, but Parliament had forbidden marriage. (i) So, "Dot" did not exactly "make way" for Adelaide (in whose honour Adelaide, Australia, was named while she was Queen(i)) but she made way for Miss Wykham. (Ed.)
6. The Reform Act of 1832, which started the reduction of patronage and venality [in the way in which Members of parliament were elected], (iii) had been resisted by the House of Lords and the "King's hostility" which he eventually, and very reluctantly, withdrew. (ii)
7. No monarch has (at least openly) been involved in politics since and although no Act is passed without "Royal Assent" that assent has never (at least publicly) been withheld. (Ed.)
8. Upon William's death from pneumonia the Spectator Magazine (London) said, by way of eulogy: "His late Majesty, though at times a jovial and, for a king, an honest man, was a weak, ignorant, commonplace sort of person." (vi)

More stuff about William IV

(i) Hilliam, David; Kings, Queens, Bones and Bastards; Sutton; Gloucestershire, England; 2001
(ii) Gardiner, Juliet, Ed; The History Today Who's Who in British History; Collins and Brown; London; 2000.
(iii) http://museumvictoria.com.au/collections/themes/2179/king-william-iv-1765-1837

QUEEN VICTORIA
"Old Vic" [1]

(1819 – 1901)
(r.1837-1901)

Silly Billy was heirless
His niece Vicky next to install
Only eighteen but mature and serene
Ready to answer the call

From years of useless Kings
The Crown was liberated
Vicky wasn't lazy, wayward or crazy
Not even pixilated!

But she'd been a lonely child [2]
Introverted and clever
The sad conclusion of so much seclusion
A lady scarred forever

So strong-willed, and stubborn
Well-ordered and nobody's fool
When decisions were taken she'd remain unshaken
Like the proverbial mule!

She married Saxe-Coburg's Albert [3]
Their union seemed fêted
An charming affair, there was love in the air
– As well as them being related [4]

Their romance was fairy tale
She adored her handsome fella
He was suave and disarming – her own Prince Charming
She was nothing like Cinderella!

He popped the question at a ball
Soon after going steady
As it transpired, no pumpkin required
She had a coach already

Albert was straight-laced [5]
Vicky rather frumpy [6]
But despite this it's seen that this King and Queen
Both loved their rumpy-pumpy

The result, of course, was offspring
A quite prodigious clan
Nine she got – a heck of a lot
Was this a clever plan?

Whether deliberate or not
Europe's Royals are populated [7]
By the children and the grandchildren
Of the kids that they created

With Albert's help and guidance [8]
She trod a new Royal path
With skill and pluck – But then tragedy struck
Bert took an early bath

At just forty one: of typhoid [9]
The tragic nitty-gritty
Was her life had no goal and her heart and soul
Gave way to deep self-pity

Years barely eased her torment
Alone she found relief [10]
Joy was rejected – and it was expected
That others would share her grief

As, indeed, they did
Throughout the population
Propriety and good form became the norm
It was a sober, dour nation

One man assuaged sad Vicky
Cheered her when she was down
Her feelings were fervent for her bold Scottish servant
Redoubtable Mr. John Brown [11]

Of ten PM's in her time
Some she'd praise, some scorn
She hated to deal with Gladstone and Peel
But liked Dizzy and Melbourne [12] [13]

Dizzy tried to change her ways
He wanted her on show
She finally said "yes" to be India's Empress
But no way would she go! 14

At the pinnacle of her reign
We were envied from Paris to Rome
Yes! – The style and vision of The Great Exhibition 15
How far had we sunk with that Dome?! 16

At Golden and Diamond Jubilees
As bells rung from spire and steeple
It was plain to see how her humility
Earned the genuine love of her people

She was Kipling's Widow at Windsor 17
As for sixty-four years she reigned on
She died as in life, a lovelorn wife
In January Nineteen-o-One

Stuff about Queen Victoria

1. Although crowned at the age of only 18 years Victoria is more often thought of today as an old lady (possibly because of the length of her reign meant she was "old" for a long time!) – hence the "nickname". (Ed.) The famous London theatre of that name was renamed in 1831 The Royal Victoria, in honour of the (then) Princess Victoria, not becoming, at least officially (it had been a local nickname)," The Old Vic" until about 1925. (i)
2. Her father, The Duke of Kent, George III's eldest son, died when she was only eight months old and she was brought up by her "protective mother" and her mother's advisor Sir John Conway being "... groomed for a rôle which was by no means certain she would take [i.e. Queen]." (ii)
3. More fully: "Prince Albert of Saxe-Coburg-Gotha. (Ed.)
4. They were first cousins. (ii)
5. Albert was "extremely strait laced and a great stickler for morality". (iii)
6. Often thought of as "frumpy" (see also "Stuff 1") Queen Victoria's attributes in her younger days have included "... beautiful, lively, full of laughter ... ready to mock ... silly prudery ..." (vi)
7. By the time of her death in 1901 Victoria's descendants "… occupied almost every throne in Europe and Russia ..." and she was known as "The Grandmother of Europe". (v)
8. Although, in the 1851 Census, Victoria shows her occupation as Queen, but Albert was listed as head of the household. (iv)
9. Albert died on 14th December 1861 and Victoria's melancholy was far from lightened by the death of her second daughter, Alice, coincidentally also on 14th December 1878. (v)
10. She wore mourning clothes for the rest of her life and lived "as a recluse on the Isle of Wight". (vi)
11. John Brown was a gillie appointed to the Royal Household in 1849 and was summoned to Osborne House (Isle of Wight) in 1864 to try to "...restore the Queen's spirits..." and they became good friends. Whether the relationship went further "the facts remain uncertain" but she was lampooned at the time as "Mrs. John Brown". The acclaimed (vii) film "Mrs Brown" did little to highlight that uncertainty. (viii)
12. "Dizzy" is a nickname of Benjamin Disraeli. (Ed.)
13. Gladstone, William Ewart: P.M. 1868 –74; 1880 – 85, 1886, and 1892 – 4; Peel, Sir Robert: P.M. 1834 – 5 and 1841 – 6; Benjamin Disraeli: P.M. 1868 and 1874 – 1880 ; Lord Melbourne (2nd Viscount Melbourne), William Lamb: P.M. 1834 and 1835 -41 (ii)
14. Although proclaimed "Empress of India" by Disraeli in 1877, and delighted with the title, Queen Victoria never visited India (many sources including (ii) and a very comprehensive newspaper article

(ix)) and she "laboured to learn Hindi" with Abdul Karim, her Munshi or teacher, (ii) who, some say, took the place of John Brown (see "Stuff 10" above) in "... her heart". (x)

15. The Great Exhibition of 1851 (seen by Victoria as Albert's own creation) included the Crystal Palace which at 1/3 mile long was then the largest enclosed space in the world. (xi)
16. There has been much criticism of many aspects of the "London" Dome. (Ed.)
17. "The Widow at Windsor" is a satirical poem by Rudyard Kipling bemoaning the soldier's lot. (ii)

More Stuff about Queen Victoria

(i)   The Old Vic Theatre Company website;
       http://www.oldvictheatre.com/about-the-oldvic/history/; and letter
       from Fliegner, S; Assistant Producer; 12th August 2012.
(ii)   Gardiner, Juliet, Ed; The History Today Who's Who in British
       History; Collins and Brown; London; 2000.
(iii) This statement appears (in quotation marks) on the website of The
       University of Victoria, British Columbia, Canada which, although it
       lists its many sources, does not say in which one this quotation
       (generally accepted as true: Ed.) is to be found.
       http://web.uvic.ca/vv/people.html
(iv)   The University of Victoria, British Columbia, Canada
       http://web.uvic.ca/vv/people.html
(v)   Wikipedia: http://en.wikipedia.org/wiki/Queen_Victoria;
(vi)   Hilliam, David; Kings, Queens, Bones and Bastards; Sutton;
       Gloucestershire, England; 2001
(vii) Gritten, D. Ed; Halliwell's Film Guide 2008: Harper Collins; London;
       2007
(viii) Mrs Brown; Miramax/Ecosse (Sarah Curtis); 1997; Great Britain
(ix)   The Nation (Pakistan) newspaper;
       http://www.nation.com.pk/pakistan-newsnewspaper-daily-english-
       online/columns/01-Jun-2012/a-tale-of-two-queens/;
(x)   BBC Radio Four series; This Sceptered Isle; Episode 66:
       15thMay2006;
       http://www.bbc.co.uk/radio4/history/empire/episodes/episode_66.sht
       ml;
(xi)   Schama, S; A History of Britain (1776 – 2000); BBC Worldwide
       Limited; London; 2002.

C. Díaz

216

EDWARD VII
"Boisterous Bertie" [1]

(1841 – 1910)
(r. 1901-1910)

Tranquil Victorian values
Hit by raging squalls
Lock up your daughters, there'll be rougher waters
After Victoria Falls

Talk about chalk and cheese
Here's Bertie her eldest lad
The wildest of blokes – so unlike his folks
He revelled in being bad!

Vicky had tried to train him
Imposing a strict regime
That patently failed and when he'd de-railed
He ached to let off steam

This was the life for Bertie
Free of Victoria's station [2]
Though it caused awful friction, his lifetime addiction
Was fun and recreation

Parties, sports and gambling
A wild social whirl
And, what's more, women galore
He adored a beautiful girl

His success with women was startling!
He'd wealth, looks and charm
Plus, he was eternally youthful – and to be quite truthful
Being King did him no harm

The scandals were truly outrageous [3]
"He caused Albert's death", Vicky claimed [4]
This was plain screwy but Bertie knew
He was first in line to get blamed

Actresses were his penchant [5]
And so's to catch their eyes
He'd visit a show and so no one would know
Turned up in heavy disguise

While watching "She Stoops to Conquer" [6]
He spied his favourite filly
"Who's that?" he cried: his friends replied
"Why that's 'The Jersey Lily'" [7]

Compared with Miss Langtry's radiance
The brightest stars were dim
Lily, the flirt, ran rings around Bert
– Then stooped and conquered him

And all this time he's married!
Alexandra at home in her rooms [8]
She knew his game and loathed to complain
Bore him five "new brooms"

His investiture to the throne
Brought more lustre to the seat
This was none too tricky – after po-faced Vicky [9]
There wasn't a fat lot to beat

Bertie was often in Europe
The Royals were his kin, after all
Through his careful advance we made peace with France
In The Entente Cordiale [10]

He backed moves to boost The Navy [11]
Our fleet had all-but gone
Thank God he was heeded – improvements were needed
Round the corner lurked World War One

The romance was over in nineteen-ten
His life had been sublime
Now the heart that bled and ruled his head
Was attacked for the very last time [12]

Perhaps this was for the best
For he was genial, peace loving and fun
A man of good grace who'd have been out of place
In the carnage soon to come. [13]

Stuff about Edward VII

1. From his full name "Albert Edward". (Ed.)
2. He was Prince of Wales from the age of 1 month to 60 years and "... largely excluded from royal duties ..." (i)
3. The quotation in "Stuff 2" above continues "... devoted his attention to society ... cited in two divorce cases ..." (i)
4. When sent to Curragh, Ireland, to train with the Grenadier Guards, he had an affair with an actress, Nellie Clifden, and Victoria attributed her husband Albert's fatal illness to the "shock and disappointment" when he heard of the relationship. (ii)
5. Actresses were certainly numbered amongst his mistresses, and included Lily Langtree (see below), Sarah Bernhardt and others less well known, but also many others, including Alice (Mrs. George Keppel) a society hostess (iii) who even visited him, with the consent of his wife (see "Stuff 8" below), Alexandra, as "... he lay dying ...". (iv)
6. "She Stoops to Conquer" was written by Oliver Goldsmith (?1730 – 1774) (possibly best known for The Deserted Village 1770 –Ed.) in 1773. (v)
7. Lillie Langtry, (1853 – 1929) starred in "She Stoops to Conquer", and was, having been born on Jersey, known as "The Jersey Lily". Her father was the Dean of Jersey. (vi) Her trademark figure was representative of the Victorian ideal with a tall, curvaceous well developed and tightly corseted figure. (vii)
8. Alexandra of Denmark (1844 – 1925) married Edward in 1863, soon after Albert's death, and did much for charity (a well-known example being the founding of "QARANC" – Queen Alexandra's Royal Nursing Corps) whilst remaining very loyal and supportive of the ever philandering Edward. (iv)
9. A little unfair perhaps, see also poem Queen Victoria, "Stuff 1" (Ed.)
10. The Entente Cordiale of 1904 was a series of agreements (largely brought about by fears about German power) between Britain and France putting an end to almost a thousand years of fighting between them. (viii) Edward certainly played a rôle, and his visits to France were "... very popular ..." (x) but the significance of that rôle can be overstated. (i)
11. "Edward played an active role in encouraging military and naval reforms, pressing for ... the modernisation of the Home Fleet." (ix)
12. He died of a heart attack and his funeral procession was led by his fox terrier Caesar, followed by Kaiser Wilhelm II and then eight European Kings. (iv)
13. World War I: around 9,000,000 dead and 15,000,000 injured. (xi)

More Stuff about Edward VII

(i) Gardiner, Juliet, Ed; The History Today Who's Who in British History; Collins and Brown; London; 2000.

(ii) Holmes, Richard; Soldiers; Harper Collins; London; 2011

(iii) http://en.wikipedia.org/wiki/Alice_Keppel

(iv) Hilliam, David; Kings, Queens, Bones and Bastards; Sutton; Gloucestershire, England; 2001

(v) Drabble, M. Ed; The Oxford Companion to English Literature; Oxford University Press; Oxford, England; 2000.

(vi) http://www.lillielangtry.com/;

(vii) http://corsetreturn.topcities.com/lillie.html;

(viii) http://en.wikipedia.org/wiki/Entente_cordiale;

(ix) http://www.royal.gov.uk

(x) /historyofthemonarchy/kingsandqueensoftheunitedkingdom/saxe-coburg-gotha/edwardvii.aspx; ("the official website of The British Monarchy");

(xi) Latimer, R.B; An Introductory History of France; John Murray; London; 1918.

(xii) Ferguson, N; The Pity of War; London; 1999.

C. Diaz

GEORGE V
"The Sailor King" [1]

(1865 – 1936)
(r.1910 – 1936)

Pity the poor Monarch
Who has to take the floor
With a grim prospect of political unrest
And impending war

To follow flighty Bertie
A grounded, sound prospect
George is shy, intense and dry
And wholly circumspect

Strict Navy life for George
And all that would entail
With his elder bro' and a tutor in tow
Just twelve when he set sail

That was the young man's life
This prince of mariners
With utmost devotion he lived a life on the ocean
For fully fifteen years!

His elder brother Albert
Would have been in line
But, as it goes he turned up his toes
Well short of twenty nine [2]

A tragedy for all concerned
Not least his fiancée
Yes, a pain in the neck for Mary of Teck
Queenly plans in disarray [3]

But she didn't have to worry
George needed a mate!
Mary was keen, he knew where she'd been
So it all turned out just great! [4]

Especially as she helped him [5]
His duties to perform
She encourages, teaches, and writes some speeches [6]
This soon became the norm

Then family time at Sandringham
He really wasn't missed
A nice wee house, slaughtering grouse
A keen philatelist [7]

Stamp out these gentle pleasures!
Smile gives way to frown
Through Palace Gates where duty waits
Beneath a thorny crown

Both George an Mary were cold and stern [8] [9]
Parents not to disobey [10]
With David they rowed, Albert was cowed [11] [12] [13]
How very wrong were they!

People mocked dour Mary
Oft as they passed by
From ear to ear she looked so severe
It's "George and the Dragon", they'd cry!

German names were infra-dig [14]
Saxe-Coburg had to go [15]
By George's edict the name "Windsor" was picked
Window dressing, don't you know!

Cruel War, then The General Strike [16]
Unrest and strife abound
So very disconcerting for this reluctant King
His miseries compound

Ill health came to haunt him
So much to endure
Lungs gone to seed from the demon weed [17]
Sea air couldn't cure [18]

He cheated death for many years
Though his health was dire
Then just before he expired of his aide he enquired
"How is The Empire?" [19]

Stuff about George V

1. He served in the navy from 1877 to 1892(i) leaving it, unwillingly, on becoming heir. (ii)
2. George's elder brother, Prince Albert Victor, Duke of Clarence and Avondale, would have become king but died in 1892, just 6 days after his 28th birthday, during an influenza epidemic in Great Britain. (ii)
3. Princess Mary of Teck (in the kingdom of Würtemburg) (iii) had become engaged to Clarence (see 2 above) only a few weeks before his death. (iv)
4. However, she married George in 1893. (iv)
5. Queen Mary supported George through the First World War, when he visited the front (once breaking his pelvis after a fall from his horse) and she visited injured servicemen. She stood by him too during his ill-health and the major political changes arising from the aftermath of the war and the rise of socialism and nationalism. (iii) (See also "Stuff 14")
6. Christmas Royal Broadcasts began in 1932 (i)
7. "George was a well-known stamp collector ... [and] ... the Royal Philatelic Collection [became] ... the most comprehensive collection of United Kingdom and Commonwealth stamps in the world ..." (ii)
8. Mary was "May" to her family, she having been born in May (1867). (iii)
9. Mary's sternness may have been encouraged by George's hatred of change such that they often both seemed like "fossils from the past". (iv)
10. They had six children, all brought up by nannies as was common in upper class families at the time, and the youngest son, Prince John, in a farm on the Sandringham Estate, "... perhaps to hide his epilepsy ...". (iii)
11. David was the name by which Edward VIII (the one who abdicated) was known. Ed. George V once allegedly spoke of him to The Archbishop of Canterbury saying: "After I am gone, the boy will ruin himself in twelve months". (iv)
12. "Rowed" as in "argued with", not as in "boat". (Ed.)
13. Albert was the name by which the later George VI was known. (Ed.)
14. Not just infra-dig, but causing real resentment, even accusations of spying, so, in 1917 George adopted the family name of Windsor. (ii) (On the eve of his wedding to Elizabeth (to be "Elizabeth II) Prince Phillip changed his name from "Battenberg" to "Mountbatten" as his maternal grandfather had done, also during WWI. (i))
15. The full name was in fact Saxe [pronounced Saxer]-Coburg Gotha. (Ed.)

16. The First World War of 1914 – 18, and the General Strike of 1926 were just two of the upheavals of the reign. (Ed.)
17. George, was a heavy smoker, as was his second son, soon to be George VI, (Ed.)
18. In 1929, during a bout of illness, George was sent to Bognor to recover and spent 13 weeks there. Sources, such as the Bognor Regis Town Council, are undecided as to whether he "graciously" bestowed the title "Regis" on Bognor or only did so after the (apocryphal?) utterance of "Bugger Bognor". By 1936 though the illness had developed too far for a sea air cure. (v)
19. Like so many "famous last words" these too may be apocryphal. (Ed.)

More Stuff about George V

(i)   Gardiner, Juliet, Ed; The History Today Who's Who in British History; Collins and Brown; London; 2000.

(ii) http://en.wikipedia.org/wiki/Prince_Albert ...;

(iii) http://en.wikipedia.org/wiki/Mary_of_Teck;

(iv) Hilliam, David; Kings, Queens, Bones and Bastards; Sutton; Gloucestershire, England; 2001.

(v)   http://www.bognor-tc.com/History.php;

EDWARD VIII
"Besot Ed"

(1894 – 1972)
(r. 1936) [1]

Now, who's this wicked playboy?
For his folks, a real trial
The antithesis of mild … the lad's running wild
Naughty, but ooooozing style!

It's David, first in line [2]
Oh, how he liked to revel!
Countless dalliances and forbidden romances [3]
The mucky, lucky, devil!

This dashing young fellow
Took many an Empire Tour [4]
And, though not blessed with brains, he piloted planes [5] [6]
And was brave in the war [7]

His flighty wings were clipped
By a domineering dame
A woman twice wed and far from purebred
Wallis Simpson, by name [8]

By her, he was smitten
Passionate and serious
Though why he'd sought out one that looked like a trout? [9]
Love can be mysterious!

Inconveniently George died!
Now King is Dave's remit
How awkward and irking it was to be working
He didn't like that, one bit! [10]

Not exactly King material
He knew that, full well
And as you now know he had in tow [11]
His real life Jezebel

He was jolly adamant
"I will have her for my bride
This is not just a 'fling', if I'm to be King
I need her by my side!"

Put her before his country!?
People were aghast
Third hand, with a drawl, this would not do at all!
Unforgivably chequered past!

His was a lone opinion
A Governments view outweighs! [12]
In under a year he was out on his ear
Three hundred and twenty five days

Should we view him harshly?
Or perhaps acquit?
'Noblesse oblige' said kowtow and ditch her now!
For love, he was deaf to it

Stuff about Edward VIII

1. The reign was so short because he abdicated, even before his coronation. (Ed.)
2. "David" was the last of his seven Christian names and that by which his parents called him. (i)
3. There was "... a series of flirtations and dalliances ...". (ii)
4. Not only were there Empire tours (as Prince of Wales) "... the biggest symbolic gesture [by the Royal Family]." was when he visited the mining villages during the depression of 1932 in Britain. (iii)
5. The implication of "a lack of brains" is a little unfair. (Ed.) By his own admission he was spared the Entrance Examination before going to Oxford University (i) and it is possible that he was more unenthusiastic, about learning, than unintelligent. (Ed. & (i))
6. He flew his first military flight in 1918 and later gained his pilot's licence. (iii)
7. Edward VIII (as Prince of Wales) was gazetted to (received a commission in) the Grenadier Guards but denied active service, by Kitchener, for fear that he should be, not killed, but captured. (i) He did however often visit the front and for that was awarded the Military Cross. (iii)
8. After his numerous "dalliances" (see "Stuff 3" above) came Mrs. Wallis Simpson (1896 – 1986) a married, previously divorced, American, by whom Edward became "mesmerised". (iv)

9. Beauty is in the eye … (Ed.)
10. As much as the job he disliked the formality and time wasting that went with those formalities (i) and many sources speak of his laxness, even missing appointments. (Ed.)
11. It was some time before the public became aware of the affair as "… the press kept the liaison secret". (Ed.) (ii)
12. The government and "Dominion leaders" would not countenance his proposed marriage, to the by then divorced again, Mrs. Simpson, so after a reign of 325 days, Edward abdicated. (ii)

More Stuff about Edward VIII

(i) H.R.H. The Duke of Windsor, K.G; The King's Story; Cassell and Co. Ltd; London; 1951.
(ii) Gardiner, Juliet, Ed; The History Today Who's Who in British History; Collins and Brown; London; 2000.
(iii) Schama, S; A History of Britain (1776 – 2000); BBC Worldwide Limited; London; 2002;

C. Díaz

GEORGE VI
"Another Bertie"

(1895 – 1952)
(r. 1936 – 1952)

Why are kids mistreated?
It makes me blooming wild!
Cruel to be kind! … Are you out of your mind!
Bertie was such a child

All too common in his young days
Even for upper classes
To chide and reprove was thought to improve
The utterly pompous asses! …

Painful callipers on his legs [1]
To correct slight knock-knees
And if he wrote left handed, sharp blows were landed [2]
Cruel, heartless, recipes

Through all his childhood days
He faced this restriction
And the sad result was a damaged adult
With an awful speech affliction [3]

Lionel Logue is chosen to help [4]
He befriends, cajoles, and teaches
With strange new ideas he allays Bertie's fears
And helps him with his speeches

At Naval College studies
Not bright … quite the opposite!
Rock bottom of the class but, eureka! … a pass! [5]
Being Royal helped a bit

A young lady stole his heart
He just knew they'd blend
She was no easy task … th-three t-t-times he'd ask
But won her in the end

The very first commoner wife
This Elizabeth Bowes Lyon
Though her blue blood for sure wasn't all that pure [6]
She'd just enough to get by on

Great tragedy now befell Bertie
In the guise of The Crown
It should not have been him, but a lovelorn whim
Caused Edward to step down [7]

Like his father before him
Conflict lay ahead
The carnage and hullaballoo of World War Two
As Europe fought and bled

He yearned to play his part
So at his insistence
He and his wife led a frugal life [8]
Symbols of National Resistance

His modus operandi?
To encourage and unite
So whenever he could, shoulder to shoulder he stood
With his subjects in their plight [9]

From war and pressure, fear and stress
Bertie deteriorates
They'd taken full toll of this delicate soul
Ajar lie the Pearly gates

Now bearing feted lungs
The foul fag so often inflicts [10]
For this enlisted man too short a span
Ex-p-pired, just f-fifty six

George was a solid, family values man
Feet firmly on the ground
A positive charge to the people at large
A jolly good egg, all round

Stuff about George VI

1. As a child he was forced to wear "painful leg splints" to correct his "knock-knees". (i)
2. Despite being naturally left-handed, he was forced to write with his right, a not uncommon practice at the time. (ii)
3. That George had a stammer is not disputed and referred to in all reference works. (Ed.)
4. Whether he, and his wife, chose the speech therapist, an Australian called Lionel Logue, or vice versa, may be a matter for conjecture depending on the source (Ed.)
5. Perhaps not quite "rock bottom" but not far off. (v)
6. His wife (to be) was Elizabeth Angela Marguerite Bowes-Lyon, daughter of Lord and Lady Glamis, but nevertheless a "commoner" marrying into royalty (iii) but when they married in 1923 there was no apparent likelihood of George (then still known as "Albert" or "Bertie") becoming king (Ed.)
7. George's elder brother, Edward, became Edward VIII but was not crowned before his abdication in 1936. (iii)
8. All things are relative (well, many, anyway) (Ed.)
9. George VI and his wife famously remained in London during WWII and although they were booed on their first visit to the East End things were very different after the bombing of Buckingham Palace and the remark of Queen Elizabeth (the later "Queen Mother") "Now I can look the East End in the face". (iv)
10. At that time the dangers of smoking were only just becoming known and many people smoked heavily (Ed).

More stuff about George VI

(iv) http://www.bbc.co.uk/history/events/george_vi_wedding
(v) Mathew, Colin,et al. (Eds); Oxford Dictionary of National Biography; Oxford University Press, Oxford, England 2007
(vi) Hilliam, D; Kings, Queens, bones and bastards; Sutton Publishing; Stroud, England 2001
(vii) Sharma, S; History of Britain (1776-2000); BBC Worldwide Limited; London 2002
(viii) http://www.willswift.com/Kinggeorge vi.htm

William I	1066-1087	House of Normandy
William II	1087- 1100	House of Normandy
Henry I	1100-1135	House of Normandy
Stephen	1135-1154	House of Blois
Henry II	1154-1189	House of Angivan
Richard	1189-1199	House of Angivan
John	1199-1216	House of Angivan
Henry III	1216-1272	House of Plantagenet
Edward I	1272-1307	House of Plantagenet
Edward II	1307-1327	House of Plantagenet
Edward III	1327-1377	House of Plantagenet
Richard II	1377-1399	House of Plantagenet
Henry IV	1399-1413	House of Lancaster
Henry V	1413-1422	House of Lancaster
Henry VI	1422-1461	House of Lancaster
Edward IV	1461-1483	House of York
Edward V	1483-1483	House of York
Richard III	1483-1485	House of York
Henry VII	1485-1509	House of Tudor
Henry VIII	1509-1547	House of Tudor
Edward VI	1547-1553	House of Tudor
Mary I	1553-1558	House of Tudor
Elizabeth I	1558-1603	House of Tudor
James I	1603-1625	House of Stuart
Charles I	1625-1649	House of Stuart
Oliver Cromwell	1649-1660	Commonwealth
Charles II	1660-1685	House of Stuart
James II	1685-1688	House of Stuart
William and Mary (jointly)	1688-1694	House of Orange
William III (alone)	1694-1702	House of Orange
Anne	1702-1714	House of Stuart
George I	1714-1727	House of Hanover
George II	1727-1760	House of Hanover
George III	1760-1820	House of Hanover
George IV	1820-1830	House of Hanover
William IV	1830-1837	House of Hanover
Victoria	1837-1901	House of Hanover
Edward VII	1901-1910	House of Saxe-Coburg-Gotha
George V	1910-1936	House of Windsor
Edward VIII	1936-1936	House of Windsor
George VI	1936-1952	House of Windsor
Elizabeth II	1952_	House of Windsor

Mnemonic Rhyme

Committing things to memory
Is often hard to do
Verses can really help the cause
I hope that this helps you!

~~~~~~~~~~~~~~~

The first two Williams and Henry
Then the only Steve
Henry Two, Richard and John
Henry Three I perceive!

Edwards One Two and Three
Then Richard the Second
Henry's Four Five and Six
Who's is next to be reckoned?

Edwards Four and Five
Richard Three thereupon
Henry the Seventh and Eighth
Edward the Sixth – soon gone!

Mary, Elizabeth, James the First
Charles's One and Two
James the Second, William and Mary
Anne who just grew and grew!

The first four Georges follow her
Then it's William Four
Victoria, Edward the Seventh
Then George the Fifth takes the floor

Edward the Eighth, George the Sixth
Ruling despite the strain
Lucky are we to have Elizabeth Two
Long may she reign!